MY LIFE

Seen Through
Our Eyes

MY LIFE
Seen Through
Our Eyes

Richard A. Brenner

SUNSTONE
PRESS

SANTA FE

Sunstone books may be purchased for educational, business, or sales
promotional use. For information please write:
Special Markets Department, Sunstone Press,
P.O. Box 2321, Santa Fe, New Mexico 87504-2321.

Book and Cover design >Vicki Ahl
Body typeface > Adobe Caslon Pro
Printed on acid free paper

———————————————————————————————

Library of Congress Cataloging-in-Publication Data
available from the publisher upon request.
ISBN 978-0-86534-848-6

———————————————————————————————

WWW.SUNSTONEPRESS.COM
SUNSTONE PRESS / POST OFFICE BOX 2321
SANTA FE, NM 87504-2321 /USA
(505) 988-4418 / ORDERS ONLY
(800) 243-5644 / FAX (505) 988-1025

Dedicated to EPB

FOREWORD

This book was started for my grandchildren, Christopher and Jacob Jackson and Alexander and Maxwell Brenner, who I realized knew nothing of my life, and Eleanor's, other than the grandparent relationship. As I started to write, I further became aware that our children, Anthony and Patricia, had big holes in their understanding of how our lives had transpired. I hope that this book will provide an additional perspective and that they will have pleasure and joy in reading about Grandy and Tai Tai.

As to others who may read this book, realize that we share with you, our family and good friends, *My Life Seen Through Our Eyes* with warmth and affection.

—Richard A Brenner
2011
Santa Fe, New Mexico

PREFACE

This is my story; not a story to impress nor a story to denigrate but a story of a boy from New Brunswick, New Jersey.

I was born June 19th, 1928 to my parents, Agnes Silverstein and Phillip Brenner. We do not know much of my father's past, since he rarely discussed it and also tended to be very reluctant in sharing that information. That might have been the way for many men who lived and married through the depression years. Why, we do not know. We do know that he was born in New York City and that his mother died when he was 20 years old. Both his parents' families had come from Germany. What happened to the family that was still in Germany, where the Holocaust killed over six million Jews throughout Europe in the concentration camps, we will never know. However, we do know that my great great great grandfather was named Max Brenner. He died in Elizabeth, New Jersey in 1801. (Maxwell Tucker Brenner was named for him and also for Eleanor's mother, Max's great grandmother whose maiden name was Tucker.)

My mother's family came from Russia and also immigrated to the United States. They had settled in New Brunswick, New Jersey. My maternal grandfather started a restaurant that prospered for many years. My mother's mother, Nettie Silverstein, was called Nana. She had five children—four girls and a boy. My mother was the eldest and her name was Agnes. Nana was to play a big part in our childhood as our mother died at a very young age, which I will discuss later. My mother and father had three boys; Terrill, Howard and me. I was the middle son and each of us is separated by five years and one month (now that's family planning). As to my early childhood, it was very warm and loving. My mother was a wonderful woman who was very caring and giving. She called me her little Robert Taylor (he was a handsome movie actor). I remember the loving care I received from her when I had scarlet fever and attacks of asthma. In those days the treatment for asthma was mustard plasters, which was hot mustard wrapped in a towel and heated and then applied to your chest. It burned like hell. I still remember this. My mother was a very good person, very giving to her family, friends and people in need. I remember one particular instance vividly. We were sitting Shiva for my mother and Mrs. Walker, a woman who had lost her husband and was left with barely any money, had three young children to raise. She told me the following: "Your mother would deliver a basket of groceries to me every week, rain or shine." My mother was also very good to her sisters. My father would give her money to buy a new dress. She shopped at the BonTon, a local store featuring ladies' apparel. She spent a quarter of the money my father gave her on a dress and would then buy each of her sisters a dress.

My most profound thought when I think of my mother is that she always made me feel special. That has always stayed with me.

Her death on February 12th, 1941 at the age of 41 was a big shock and a shattering experience to me. Several months before she was at a Bar Mitzvah reception and tripped while dancing the Horah, fell to the floor, and was accidentally kicked in the nose. She suffered excruciating headaches from that time and doctors were not able to determine the cause. She most probably had a cerebral hemorrhage, which now, can generally be taken care of. My father had sent her to Florida to recover. She had an attack and died. I was on a Boy Scout hike at Farrington Lake and was dropped off on my return, near my home. When I turned the corner I saw that my house was surrounded by cars and crowded with people. I remember running up the terrace to our front porch where a friend of the family turned to me and said "Dick, your mother is dead."

I was 12 years old at the time and my Bar Mitzvah had been scheduled for June. It was an extremely difficult and sad event because of my mother's death. I vividly remember my father working with me on my Bar Mitzvah portions and my speech. He took me to the temple (Anshe Emeth) where he instructed and rehearsed me, constantly saying: "A comma means a pause and a period means a stop" in order to avoid my racing in both my reading of the Torah and my Bar Mitzvah speech. (This cautioning of comma and period I have used often with my children and grandchildren with great results.) My father also insisted that my brothers and I attend Friday night service every week to say Kaddish (prayers for the dead) for one year and to visit the cemetery, which we did.

My father was a self-made man and was a very prominent and well-respected citizen in New Brunswick, New Jersey. He was president of the temple, the Jewish Community Center, and the past exalted ruler and trustee of the Elk's Lodge, etc. etc. He was a well known and well thought of judge. His funeral took place on an extremely snowy day with near blizzard conditions, but in spite of the weather 900 people attended his memorial service. The temple could not hold all the people and many stood outside in the snow during the service. He was 61 years old, too young for this good man, when he died from a heart attack on December 2nd, 1957. I was 29 years old at that time and had married my wonderful wife, Eleanor, the year before. (More about that later.)

My father attended Rutgers University and New Jersey Law School graduating with honors. He was the Honor Man at the New Jersey Law School and passed the bar examination nine months prior to graduation from night law school (which was quite an achievement).

While still attending night school, he married my mother on December 26th, 1920. During law school he taught at several New Jersey schools and worked in the swamps between Newark and New York City. While working in the swamps, to save money, he ate rice pudding because he knew the Orientals subsisted on rice as the backbone of their diet and in addition it was satisfying and very filling. As he prospered he never ate rice pudding again. I am enclosing a letter that my father sent to his relatives in Germany, dated August 25th, 1929, which describes the "crushed derby" incident where he was nearly killed; in addition it gives a timely and colorful picture of this period.

August 25th, 1929
My dear Uncle Hermann and Aunt Gustel:

A long time has passed since I last wrote a letter to you, not because we have forgotten you but rather for the reason that many events have occurred which just caused us to postpone writing to you. We have received your several post cards and letters, the latter containing the photograph, and we are joyed that you are all in good health.

I presume that you received the post card which we sent to you on the Graf Zeppelin. I am writing this letter intending likewise to mail the same on the Zeppelin which is scheduled to arrive at Lakehurst within a day or two. The world is marveling at its successful flight.

Since I last wrote you, many things have arisen which have kept us all occupied, including the illness of both children for two months, and also myself. I thank God as I write this letter that I am here to do so. On the evening of April 1st I was attending a dinner in New York City given in honor of a prominent Jewish jurist. Returning to New Brunswick, I drove an automobile owned by another attorney, and we were traveling on a newly constructed highway. It was a windy evening, and suddenly without any warning of danger, all danger lights and signals having been blown out by the wind, we came to the end of the pavement, and a drop of several feet into a gully below. I quickly realized our danger, and endeavored to avoid what appeared sure and certain death, but I was unable to bring the automobile to a stop. Our car, with both of us inside, fell into the gully, and truned (sic) over twice, finally coming to a stop with the roof on the ground and the wheels in the air. The weight of the chassis caused the roof to crash, and almost instantly the entire front of the car was ablaze. In order to escape I kicked at one of the glass doors, breaking the window and we crawled out. Neither of us sustained serious injuries, our suffering being nervous shock and bruises on the body. It was Divine Providence that spared our lives, and we thank God for his blessings.

I am again in good health, and am happy to say that both of the children are again well, and that Agnes also is enjoying the best of health.

(It is important to add that we were both wearing derbies, which are stylish, very hard hats, that cushioned the blow to our heads when the roof collapsed.)

Agnes and I are planning to make a week-end trip to the races at Saratoga, New York State from Friday until Tuesday. It will be the first time that we shall leave the children, and while we are anticipating the short vacation, we regret to leave the youngsters behind. Our youngest, Richard, has just learned to walk, and he is at an age at which he requires constant attention. However, my mother in law lives a few doors from our home, and one of Agnes's sisters has promised to stay with the maid and the children.

One of Bertha's babies died. The other, a boy, is now getting along very nicely as is Bertha. Eddie's wife expects to give birth to a baby within a few weeks. Evelyn is also well and happy.

Whenever we receive letters or cards, and

particularly photographs from you, it makes us very happy. So much the more because we can see in your photographs that you are all in good health and apparently happy. I have asked to have a photograph made of herself and the children, and as soon as this is done, the first photo will go forward to you.

Our Gina is quite a splendid looking young lady—in fact, she is similar to our American flappers— pretty and attractive. I cannot tell you how anxious we are to see you all in person.

Please convey my warmest regards to Herr Max Marcus. I do not of course remember him as I was a small las when we visited Germany.

We are always anxious to have Gina send us a few lines with your letters. I am able to read the German script, and it is a source of my greatest pleasure to receive your letters. I hope that you have no difficulty in having my letters translated. If you desire, I can have my letters written in the German language, but typewritten in English script. I shall do so with my next letter.

I shall write you again within a few days. We send our love and kisses to you all, Uncle Herman, Aunt Gustel, and Cousins Eddie and Gina, and hope this letter will find you all happy and healthy.

Your nephew,

Phillip

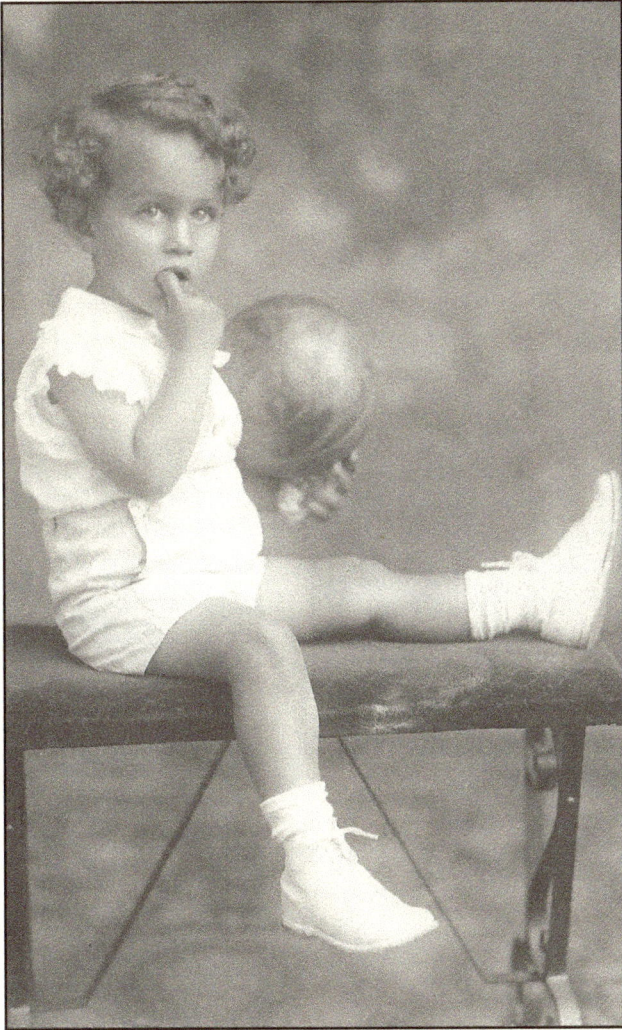

Richard Arthur Brenner: two years old

Dicky: three years old

Dicky: 4 years old

GROWING UP

After my mother died in 1941, my grandmother moved in with us at 16 Llewellyn Place and stayed for almost two and a half years. Terry was in the armed forces. Nana was very good to me and my younger brother, Howard. Helping to raise two young boys was very hard work. She was neither a fun person nor a very happy person, and it must have been very difficult for my father. In 1943, my father met a woman, Rita Ruby, and they subsequently married. Rita had two grown girls, Bette who was married to Larry Gluckin, and Jeanne. Jeanne lived with us as she was divorced. She later married Herman Robinson. My father legally adopted Bette and Jeanne. Jeanne changed her name, officially, to Jeanne Brenner. Jeanne and Bette were wonderful to me and were very important influences in my life. Certainly, Bette was a major player, and throughout the rest of her life, we were very close and I was a source of strength and support for her.

Rita was a difficult person. She was always on stage and called herself Duchess (which she surely acted like). You would sit down at the dinner table and she would start a story and at the end of dinner she would still be telling the same story and no one could interrupt. She was very manipulative and devious and created a lot of pressure and anxiety. I was very happy to go off to college. In 1960, three years after my father's death, Rita moved back to New York City and was to create some marital problems for me that I shall go into at a later point.

While in high school, I worked Thursday nights and Saturdays at Mile's Shoe Store. This was a lower priced operation and I can tell you some awfully dirty feet came into the store. When I would see an exceptionally dirty person I would visit the stock room to avoid having to help them. When I was a senior in high school, I also worked at Rutgers University, in the library. I was working there the day that President Roosevelt died. It was a sad moment for the country, since he had led us through the depression as well as most of WWII.

Dick at Cedar Lake Camp: Milford, Pennsylvania, 1935

Several references during my growing up period must be mentioned, since they were an important part of this period. First was my love affair with summer camps beginning when I started sleep-away camp the summer immediately after my fifth birthday in June. I was by far the youngest kid in camp and I remember my older brother Terry paying special attention to me so that I would not be homesick. I loved the competition and camaraderie and over the years I was a camper, waiter, junior counselor, color war leader (this is where the camp is split into two groups that compete for one week in all competitive aspects possible in camp life) and basketball counselor. I went off every summer from age five to 21. This was a period when I was fanatic about basketball and ended up playing for my high school team. My father had a photograph of me in my basketball uniform, in a player's stance, which he proudly displayed on his desk. (I helped my grandsons, Alex and Max, learn how to shoot a basketball and make a driving layup.) One night coming home from an away game I forgot my keys to the house. No one was up and I made a snowball and threw it against my younger brother, Howard's, window to wake him up. I managed to throw the snowball through the window and woke up everybody in the house. During the war period, Howard and I did a lot together from basketball to our usual Sunday night dinner at the Lido Gardens, a Chinese restaurant. The owner was a client of my father's.

Dick in those plus fours: Look at those knickers, 1940

One summer we were all at the same camp, Blue Mountain, and my brother Terry was a waiter and Howard and I were campers. There was a softball game between the waiters and the counselors. The catcher for the counselors was Hal Zastrow who was a college football star playing linebacker or tackle for Temple University. No one had ever knocked him over! Then Terry was rounding 3rd base and Zastrow was blocking the plate and for sure it was going to be a close play at home plate. Well, Zastrow caught the ball, knowing he would have to tag Terry out. Terry was racing towards Zastrow, the catcher, and then the big collision. Zastrow held onto the ball for the out and Terry laid there with a dislocated shoulder, but he had knocked the catcher totally over.

Another experience was that I thought Don Hudson, who was the receiver for the Green Bay Packers, was the greatest. I had seen the game on November 22nd, 1942, where he scored 21 points: it was a tie with the Giants, 21 to 21. He kicked three points after touchdowns and caught three touchdown passes, earning all his team's points. Inspired by this, I decided to make up a game where I had Howard throw the football to me and I'd jump in front of the windows in the garage, simulating a defender and trying to catch the pass. Of course, we broke the window. My father didn't notice this for months, and when he did notice it we acted very surprised and said it must have been broken a while ago.

My senior year in high school was in 1946, right after the war ended. The gym program was run by a former Major in the U.S. Rangers. Thus, it was body building time. We played tackle football on the wood gym floor without protective equipment. Wow, this was rough and painful! Another game: one team was given the ball in the center circle and the other team had to get it out and anything goes. You can just imagine the fighting, punching and kicking that went on! We also had to run an obstacle course and dive off the bleachers into a chain formed by my fellow students and be thrown in the air until you got to the end of the line. One of the toughest kids I ever knew was a kid named Petie Clark whom the Italians did not like. The Italians got to the end of the line and threw him up in the air about ten feet and stepped aside and let him bounce off the floor. He hit really hard and was knocked out. (Some fun!)

The Brenner Boys: Howard, Richard, and Terrill

Dick in his basketball player's stance: 1944

COLLEGE YEARS

My first experience with anti-Semitism was apparent when I applied to Dartmouth College. Dartmouth required you to have an alumni interview before you were accepted. My father drove me to the interview in New Jersey one evening and waited outside in his car. The interview was very negative about my fitting into Dartmouth life, and particularly so after the interviewer read the section where you stated your religious preference. I do not remember the exact language, but he definitely made his point. I remember coming out of the interview and telling my father that I did not want to attend Dartmouth and they probably wouldn't accept me as I was Jewish.

I matriculated at the University of Pennsylvania, the famous Wharton School, in 1946. The war had just ended the previous year. My class was 50 percent veterans and 50 percent public, private and prep school kids. My freshman dorm, where I lived during my first year, was named Cleeman. I was on the fourth floor with about six other freshmen all having been in the service and ranging in rank from a captain to an ensign. I was the greenest, youngest kid on the block. The first thing the ex-military group did was take me to Smokey Joes to drink beers. After this first drinking session I wobbled back to my dorm with them. The next day, after taking my first quiz in the Industrial Management course and receiving a zero grade, I figured I would never be able to survive. I gave up the midweek beers and carousing and by the time I graduated I had a very high academic record and was elected to Beta Gamma Sigma. Beta Gamma Sigma represents academic achievement in business schools and is the equivalent of Phi Beta Kappa. I was also elected to Pi Gamma Mu, a social science honorary society.

Dick at Camp Navaho: counselor, 1946

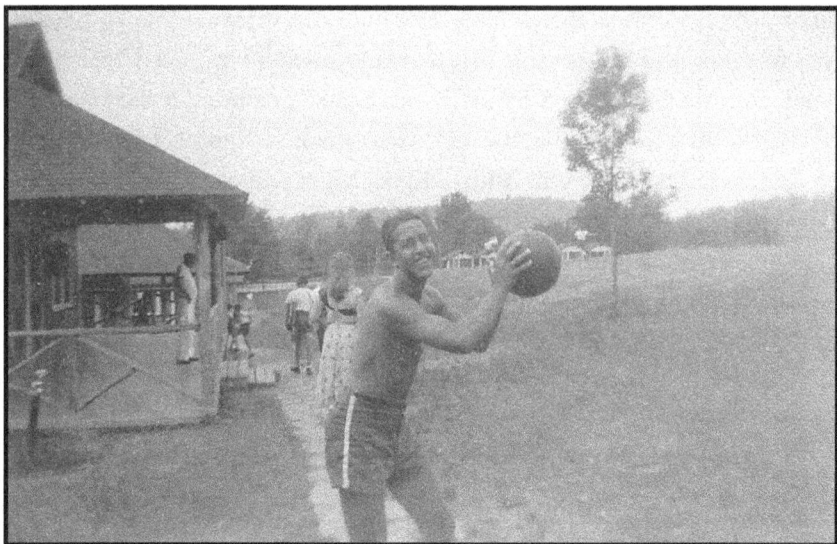

My time at college was wonderful and I matured a great deal. I joined a fraternity, Phi Epsilon Pi, which helped to make the university and big city of Philadelphia smaller and much more intimate and warmer. At a class party for the freshman, shortly after classes began, I met a very pretty and charming freshman girl, Peggy Liebfried, whom I invited to my first big fraternity pledge party. It was a magical evening and we both fell madly in love. Our evening together ended at about three o'clock in the morning. When I went to call her several days later I received the cold shoulder. I called three or four more times and I finally got the message that she did not want to see me or go out with me. I did not learn until June of that year, from Don Swan, who was a friend of hers, that the reason she did not go out with me was because the sorority she was pledging did not permit the girls to go to a Jewish fraternity. To her credit, she resigned from her sorority, but it was too late to rekindle the romance.

Several interesting events occurred while I was in college. One was my setting up a small business where I made quite a bit of extra money that I very much needed. My tuition and room and board were paid for, but I was not given an allowance. My brother-in-law, Herman Robinson, owned Boaz, a paper box company, that supplied local florists. In the years that I was in college, there were many, many formal dances and parties at all the fraternities. (As I remember, there were over 25 fraternities at the University of Pennsylvania.) All the guys would present their dates with corsages, mostly orchid corsages, when they picked them up for the dance or the "big party." In my freshman year, I recruited a member from each fraternity to sell corsages. I then contacted a local florist, whom Boaz sold to, and made a deal with them to sell bulk orders of corsages to me at wholesale prices instead of the retail prices that would have been charged for an individual order. On Monday, Tuesday and Wednesday I collected the corsage orders from each representative at the different fraternities. On Thursday I would place my order, and on Fridays I delivered the orchids to the fraternity representatives. My profit was already built into the price that I charged each representative. They, in turn, added on their commission to the individual purchasing the corsage. Everyone was happy. Why? Because the individual purchaser of the corsage did not pay any more than he would have paid at retail and he did not have the bother of calling the florist to order the corsage, nor going to the florist to pick up the corsage. It was delivered directly to him. The fraternity rep made his commission, and I made my profit right off the top. It was a win-win situation. In addition to making money during my four years at Wharton, this endeavor also gave me some business experience.

As an aside, there was a funny experience that I had at a traditional Ivy Ball Weekend. I invited a girl from Harrisburg, Pennsylvania, to be my date. She was young, 17 years old. I hardly knew her, having just met her several weeks before. But not having a date, my friends pressured me to find one. Since she was very pretty and had a nice personality, I thought we might have a great weekend.

On the Thursday before Ivy Weekend, I was in a boxing match. I thought I was winning the fight until I got clobbered on the left side of my nose and blood was gushing all over. I was sent to Student Health who said the nose was broken and they would fix it. They surely did; they placed a steel rod up my nose and went, "bam!" and snapped the rod across my nose and said, "Now it's fixed." (Little did I know that this would be the first of four broken noses that I was to sustain.)

My date arrived Friday afternoon and our plans were to drive to Atlantic City for the evening, a distance of 60 miles. The car was very crowded so she sat on my lap and I was only concerned she not back into my nose, so I had my hand on her back the whole way there and back. I survived the Friday night trip but the best was yet to come.

The big event of the weekend was a formal dinner and dance at my fraternity house. All the girls were in long gowns with corsages (which I had sold to my fraternity brothers). My date made her entrance down the stairs, and her front tooth, which had been capped, fell out. So there we were, me with a broken nose and she without a front tooth. I thought the situation was very humorous. She did not appreciate my humor and broke out in hives. Now there's a memory!

During high school and college, basketball was a major passion of mine. I did not make the Penn basketball team since the coach of the football team was also the coach of the basketball team and he put the football players on the team so they would have free board (food) between freshman and sophomore football seasons. After class, one of the fellows I played basketball with, Jack McClosky, had been a four letter man as a freshman but was disqualified from collegiate sports in his sophomore year because he had played semi-pro baseball during that summer. He later went on to become the general manager of the Detroit professional basketball team, the bad boys (Dennis Rodman, etc.) who won several NBA championships.

The college years flew by and during one of the summer vacations, I visited my roommate Merlin Behrend Hagedorn (nicknamed "Bunny") in Gadsden, Alabama. It was an awakening for me since I had never been in the Deep South and saw how different it was from the northeast. It also was my first commercial airline flight at the age of twenty. (My, has the world changed!) Bunny's grandfather lived in Philadelphia and was a wonderful man. A renowned surgeon, tennis player, and the owner of one of the first cars in Philadelphia. I had dinner with Bunny and Dr. Behrend on many occasions and had my first "bout" with oysters at one of these dinners. Since that time, I have not eaten an oyster.

CHOICES

I was coming to the end of my college career and realized certain facts: a) there was no family business to go into (probably lucky for me since many of those situations don't work out); b) I did not want to return to New Brunswick, New Jersey (too confining); c) I did not want to be a lawyer or doctor, toward which my father kept pushing me. Even at my graduation from Penn he talked about it not being too late to become a lawyer. My father felt that a profession put you one step further up on the ladder to success. I knew that I wanted to go into business and felt that retailing would provide an excellent experience and background for whatever I might decide to do later in life.

During my senior year in college I took a marketing course taught by Dr. Ralph Breyer. He was a very interesting man and he was totally deaf. He announced this the first day in class and said that he worked with his wife who listened to him talk to make sure he was speaking clearly since he did not hear his own voice. He also read lips and could ask relatively simple questions that did not involve long explanations. He was a great teacher with fantastic exuberance and enthusiasm for his subject. He mentored me to go into retailing, where he thought the experience would be useful for the rest of my working career, and it certainly was. I am indebted to Dr. Breyer for this and have a warm and appreciative feeling toward him for his knowledge, communication skill and dedication to his students. He wrote exemplary letters of recommendation for me to the potential jobs I was seeking in retailing. I joined Bloomingdale's Junior Executive training program in August of 1950. I was to work there from 1950 to 1967, rising from a Junior Executive to a Senior Merchandise Manager. Originally, I was paid 50 dollars per week and managed to live in New York City (how I do not know). My college roommate and I survived for a year living at Seventieth Street and West End Avenue in a ground floor apartment and sharing a bathroom with some good-time girls.

BLOOMINGDALE YEARS

My first position was in the Junior Executive training program, where for six months you were farmed out to different areas to gain experience as to what kind of department and merchandise you had a preference for—i.e. home furnishings or ready-to-wear. My first assignment was in the housewares area which was on the sixth floor. I was determined to get ahead quickly, but knew nothing about department stores. I asked the D.S. (Division Supervisor) who was a low level management person (did I know?) what I could do to be of extra help. She said at the end of the day I could close all the windows, which were open (there was no air conditioning then), for this huge corner, sixth floor department. I said sure, and by so doing continually missed my train to New Brunswick, as I was commuting every day at that time, and had to wait an extra hour before I reached home. (Anything to get ahead? I roomed in New York City with Bunny starting that September.)

The training squad was fun. There were about 15 of us, half men and half women. Several were very pretty girls from Wellesley, Vassar and Smith college. We dated a lot. My second assignment was in the boys department in the basement as an assistant buyer. This was quite an experience as every week all the regular merchandise had to be replaced with sale merchandise. I would dream about folding underwear, sweaters, pants and shirts. The buyer never dirtied his hands by pitching in. One of my Thursday and Saturday employees, who was the best folder I had ever seen, was to become president of Saks Fifth Avenue, Bob Suslow. I learned one important thing in this department. Namely, all the sales help was older, probably 50 and up, and at that time seemed very elderly to me. I quickly learned it was imperative for them to take care of housekeeping (i.e. straightening up the stock), otherwise I would be buried alive. How to reach them and accomplish this was the question. I realized that with this task they did not have the same motivation I had, and that each person was completely different. Therefore, one I had to push and the other pull and another "schmooze" and on and on. This was a great lesson in how to deal with an individual and bring out the best in each of them.

Subsequently, I became a buyer. My first department was Department 931, which was a robe and low-priced dress operation. The previous buyer was Ed Meyers, who was to become president of Grey Advertising. As an aside, I had a big romance with his sister, Ann, a serious artist. When I took over this department it was losing a great deal of money and within one year I turned it around to make a great deal of money. This experience taught me the power of mark-up thus resulting in potentially high gross margin. That means taking the cost price and determining the initial selling price, the difference being the mark-up. I also made a merchandise decision when I was a buyer that stood me well over the years—namely that when selecting styles from a collection I should only buy those styles that I really liked and coined the expression "when in doubt, leave it out." This was applicable as well to later investment decisions and other important decisions where I had to make a choice.

Gross margin is the key number that controls bottom line profits. The importance of mark-up is that it determines your profit on that item. The mark-up multiplied by the number of items sold determines the total mark-up. From this, mark-downs and other more minor deductions (such as freight) reduce the margin. The result is gross margin, from which all other costs and expenses are deducted to determine the final operating profit or loss. It's what covers a multitude of sins and errors and obviously the greater the gross margin the greater the profit potential. This concept of high mark-up was inherent in all the operations I was involved with and was responsible for the financial profits made in our own business as well as the Wall Street companies that I was to work with in years to come.

I must tell a very funny story that is quite visual. When I was a buyer for the robe department, there were bargain tables set up in the center of the busiest selling floor. These huge tables gave an opportunity for a buyer to sell off-price and promotional merchandise. One day I was filling in additional robes for the sale table since they were selling quickly. I loaded myself with robes and could barely see over the top of them. It was necessary to carry them up an escalator. Suddenly, I was spread eagle at the top of the escalator over a screaming woman who had caught the heel of her shoe in the escalator. I landed on top of her with all the robes. It wasn't a pretty picture. Another time I merchandised a two-dollar sale of dresses that were originally priced at five to ten dollars. The reaction from our ad was unbelievable and we practically had a riot. We sold thousands of these dresses.

In 1951, I moved into 110 East 31st Street with Melvin Jacobs, who was much later to become president of Saks Fifth Avenue. We lived on the top floor of a fourth-floor walk-up with very steep steps. The apartment was so old that the door lock consisted of a bar that ran at a right angle from the floor to the door. The kitchen was the size of a tiny closet. In 1954, Mel and I were both buyers and we were becoming more successful. We decided to move uptown to 208 East 51st Street. This was really progress since we were in a much nicer apartment and on the second floor of a brownstone. Mel had a girlfriend and was not in the apartment very often, and thus my younger brother, Howard, who was at Yale, had a great place to stay when he visited New York City.

In 1954, not only did I move into this apartment, but I also bought my first car. It was a blue Chevrolet BelAir convertible. The car was great and I kept it for many years. It was quite a thrilling purchase at the time, being my biggest to date, and represented to me a major step forward on the ladder of my success. In those days you were able to park on the streets of New York City and did not have to garage your car. Today to park your car in a garage costs close to 40 dollars a day in Midtown and 600 dollars and up for a monthly space on the Upper East Side.

Living on East 51ˢᵗ Street, we were able to walk to work under the Third Avenue EL, an elevated train, which had not as yet been taken down. The EL was a subway/train monstrosity which kept Third Avenue very dark and dingy as well. The EL was supported by steel girders and columns that supported the train tracks. The removal of the EL (girders, columns, tracks, etc.) dramatically opened up Third Avenue since it was a wide and beautiful street. It became a major Avenue in New York City and Bloomingdale's was the only major store on the Upper East Side at that time. Bloomingdale's management determined the affluent population of New York City was moving uptown to the east side and Bloomingdale's had the prime location. Bloomingdale's then merchandised to capture this customer, eliminating major appliances and lower-priced merchandise and replacing them with designer and upscale merchandise.

As a merchandise manager I had many departments reporting to me and I was responsible for their performance. My favorite buyer was a beautiful blonde lady, named Grace, who was charming, as well as pretty, and a pleasure to work with. I had to make one of the most difficult decisions of my career. Her department was not performing as it should have, and it was losing a great deal of money. To overcome this, I planned to move a hungry and aggressive buyer into a much more important position. It was very difficult for me to terminate this buyer because of my personal feelings for her. However, this decision resulted in a 100 percent turn-around for this department and it became one of the most profitable in the entire store. Often, a very painful decision works toward the greater good for the company and should be made at the earliest possible time. This is a leader's responsibility. It requires you to evaluate people fairly and objectively and to handle situations with great sensitivity. You must be careful in your consideration of people since you see only pimples on your own employees, whereas someone from the outside may look better simply because you do not know their faults.

I was promoted many times at Bloomingdale's since I had excellent taste, strong number skills, and worked well with people. During my career there I worked for various senior vice presidents. Two of them stand out. Harold Krensky was one of the best "people persons" I have ever known. He had the rare ability of making each individual he was talking to feel as if they were the most important person in the world to him. He took this talent to the presidency of Federated Department Stores. In addition, I learned that helping people solve their business problems not only made them more productive at their job but also helped me to become more successful. The other senior vice president I reported to I found to be very small minded with limited vision. He tended to procrastinate and had trouble making a positive decision to go forward and would always favor the old tried and true method. I learned from this situation that I could be too independent and forceful in pushing my agenda when someone was not open to change and progress. This experience contributed to causing me to look forward to other opportunities.

EARLY MARRIED LIFE

While I was a merchandise manager in the famous Bloomingdale's basement, called the downstairs store by the president of the store, I met Eleanor Meyerson Wesley. It was the single best thing about my Bloomindales experience. Eleanor had graduated from N.Y.U., Phi Beta Kappa and cum laude. She was to become my wife and soulmate for 54 years at the time of this writing. She has brought great joy and happiness to my life, and I will save this love story for later, to cover in greater detail.

I did not get married until I was 28, but on one occasion I came very close. I had been deeply involved with one young woman for several years, spending weekends at her parents' home in Scarsdale and seeing her several times during the work week. I asked my sister Bette to go with me to pick out an engagement ring. We were in the jewelry store looking at rings, and all of a sudden I turned to my sister and said, "What am I doing here? I do not want to spend the rest of my life with her." We left the store and that night I broke up with her. It was rather messy and very difficult and for several months thereafter she called members of my family to try to resurrect the relationship to no avail. I came away learning what I needed in a wife. I knew that I needed a warm and loving woman as well as a charming and pretty person. That led me to Eleanor, who had all those qualities that I felt I needed. What great luck and good fortune. I cannot imagine my life without her.

I believe marriage is probably the single most important decision one makes and that you should carefully consider your specific needs. Marriage is not a straight line upward but is rather like a stock with peaks and valleys. If one gets through the valleys your marriage is stronger than ever. Also, after you live together for many years, you gain a greater understanding of that person. Translated, that means you try to avoid pushing the other person's hot buttons.

Eleanor and I were officially married December 19th, 1956, and we went to Europe on our honeymoon. I had given her a choice of an engagement ring or a trip; she selected the trip to Europe. Eleanor had been married to another man at 17. We had to wait for her divorce to become legal in New York State, so we actually eloped on Saturday October 6th, 1956. We were accompanied by Bette and Larry Gluckin, my sister and brother-in-law, who were to serve as our witnesses and best man and lady. We eloped to Greenwich, Connecticut, where Eleanor's divorce was legal, and were married by a justice of the peace named Jacob Weiss. We spent our first married night at the Boston Clock Inn (a charming cottage) that was part of Stonehenge. We had dinner with Bette and Larry and then retired to our cottage. We returned to New York City the following day, to my bachelor apartment at 1040 Park Avenue. We told no one, other than Bette and Larry, who of course were with us at our marriage. My best friend, Bob Block, was on a date that Sunday night and after dropping off his date well past midnight, decided to drop in on me. The doorman would not let him enter the building and told him that I had just been married. A shocked Bob did not at all believe what he had just heard. So, in the early morning of Monday, I received a phone call and verified that Eleanor and I were now a married couple. Was Bob ever surprised!

OUR HONEYMOON
TRIP TO EUROPE

The flight we took to London, the first stop on our European journey was late to depart and we were unable to fly directly to London as planned and had to refuel at Shannon, Ireland. Our travel agent had told us that we were to have a suite during our layover at the Shannon Airport Hotel. We actually had two tiny, cell-like rooms, furnished with army cots and no heat. (This is a suite?) Down a very, very long hall was a freezing communal bathroom with an ice water shower, sink and toilet.

When we finally landed in London, it rained that true, constant, nonstopping London winter hard drizzling rain and continued to do so for the next four days. Rain or no rain, London was fascinating. On the first morning we realized I needed some warmer clothing. Off to Harrods we went. Eleanor was ready to go to work buying (not shopping). Our first stop was the men's department of Harrods. Within the hour, Eleanor had convinced me I needed brown suede walking boots, two cashmere sweaters, a tweed hunting jacket with suede patches at the elbows, a cashmere scarf and a Burberry tartan-lined rain coat. She kissed me in front of Harrod's staff, who were quite embarrassed, and said "Darling, these are presents for you from me." (To this date she has not changed; many are better than few.)

We had a whirlwind four days walking the streets of London, visiting the wonderful British Museums, Buckingham Palace and the changing of the guard and going to theatre.

Theatre in London was superb. The plays we saw were brilliantly acted and there was an additional plus that Eleanor adored. It was the British custom to serve tea at intermission. The tea lady, a matron in black, served each of us at our seat with our own china tea pot, cup, saucer, sugar bowl and milk pitcher on an individual porcelain tray. Eleanor was enchanted. I was happy also, because the tea was very hot and the theatre had no heat and I was really cold even in my new sartorial splendor.

Eleanor had to see everything and go everywhere, including the flower market where she was sure we would see an Eliza Doolittle. We didn't! But, I bought her a bouquet of violets from a toothless old hag. Every day, after theatre and before dinner we raced back to the hotel for a joint hot, hot bath. It truly was the only way to be warm and cozy except for being in bed.

On our flight to Paris, we were in a prop plane. No one had informed us that the prop planes in 1956 sometimes stalled and dropped a few thousand feet very quickly and suddenly. We clutched each other's hand, not breathing at all until the engines caught again and the plane was able to once again reach an acceptable altitude.

Our hotel in Paris was exceptional. It was The Bellman on Rue Francois Premier et Marbeouf. Eleanor fell in love, not only with the hotel, but with the tiny brass gated elevator, our coffee and croissants in bed, the shops, the quaint restaurants, Montparnasse, Versailles, le Jeu de Paume, the Bois de Boulogne, the Louvre, Rue de Rivoli, Rue St. Germain, the Champs Elysse, le Tour Eiffel, le Rive Gauche, le Rive Droit, le Seine, le Bateau Mouche, the tiny boulangeries, the patisseries, and ultimately, Notre Dame. In Paris I gained a perspective on how old Paris was as we walked through the streets and compared the buildings to the United States, which then seemed like a very young country in comparison. It was a completely different feeling. On the very snowy Christmas Eve of 1956 we went to Notre Dame and then through the falling snow walked back to our hotel along the river bank. How romantic can you get? Tony was conceived that night.

Before we had left the United States, Eleanor had seen 24 karat gold china at Tiffany's. She asked me to have it researched by our Associated Merchandising Corporation (AMC) office in Paris. (AMC was a conglomerate of many of the most outstanding retail stores in America that, ideally, had joint buying power to achieve discounts and special, exclusive merchandise from all over the world. The retail stores that were represented by AMC, because of their greater buying power, were able to often achieve much lower cost prices on the selected items. Also, where merchandise did not exist and the demand was there, AMC was often able to fill that void.) We found out that the china Eleanor coveted was made in Paris by M. Le Tallec. She insisted that his being in Paris was just fortuitous and that we should find him, which indeed we did. He lived on the outskirts of Paris in a section called Montparnasse. His home, which was on the second floor of his factory, had an eight foot tall wall surrounding the property. At first he was cold and aloof but when Eleanor spoke to him in French he started to loosen up and he saw our exuberance about his collection. He showed us his historical watch ring collection (watches mounted on a ring and hidden by jeweled lids) and we were flabbergasted by it. The most amazing, to Eleanor, was the ring-watch that Napoleon had given to Josephine. This collection, he told us, was going to be exhibited at Tiffany's in New York City in about two to three months from the time we saw it, which it was.

After our opening salvo with the rings he was thrilled to show us around the studio and factory. The factory was manned by creative artists who handpainted his designs on Limoges china. Limoges is one of the great European china producers. I neglected to mention that the dishes we were looking at were all 24 karat gold and absolutely spectacular; however, each piece cost a small fortune. Eleanor's father had given her an unlimited letter of credit for our wedding gift. We ended up buying this spectacular set of fourteen place settings from M. Le Tallec, putting the letter of credit to good use. Each dish had the following logo on its reverse side:

"Designed and Painted Entirely by Hand for Madame Eleanor Brenner by M. Le Tallec, Paris" (in French). It was probably a foolish purchase, in that the china was so extravagant and elegant, we used it probably only two or three times in our 54 years of marriage. It also suffered some breakage and disrepair when we stored it in a New York City warehouse while we were building our permanent home in Santa Fe, New Mexico. I do not know what will eventually become of this gold china, but in looking back it was then that I realized that women are different from men and have a far longer vision and horizon. Men always seem to be catching up.

Next on our tour of Europe, we went to Rome which was wonderful. We spent New Year's Eve at a Roman night club. We were the only non-Italian people at this night club, and the management as well as the guests really fussed over us. They called Eleanor "principessa," and she truly looked like one in her strapless black lace dress and her gold pleated Balmain evening coat. After three hours, the men started dancing with each other and throwing dishes into the fireplace. I told Eleanor it was definitely time to leave.

We moved on to Florence, Italy, where we stayed at a small charming hotel. We went shopping and found a beautiful, ornate sterling silver water pitcher by Hugo Bellini, which I proceeded to buy. Eleanor was thrilled. The pitcher was heavily chased and it became the standard for serving water at our dinner table all of our married life. It is about seventeen inches in height and its capacity to hold water is very large. We were afraid to have this shipped so we had it crated in wood. It was some huge package after its crating and I schlepped this everywhere for the remainder of our honeymoon. However, we have enjoyed pouring water from it for 54 years.

After Florence we traveled to Switzerland, where we spent several days. We were stranded in Geneva, as there was an inversion of air with heavy clouds that blocked any fresh air from reaching the ground. Eleanor was sick with asthma so I suggested we take the train to Barcelona, Spain. We met a Turkish couple on the train and played bridge all the way to Barcelona. It was my first time playing bridge. The Turkish lady, Nemin, was my partner and a virtual killer. Nemin insisted we play for money. Her husband, Veshti, was charming and a graduate of Columbia University in architecture. Eleanor had played bridge while at college and she said Veshti was a very good bridge player. She said, "How you and Nemin won every rubber was either a miracle or low down cheating!" Obviously, Nemin never lost, no matter what she had to do.

After Barcelona, we visited the Canary Islands, which were fascinating, since the beach was volcanic rock and the entire resort sat on a volcanic formation. We met two charming young men at our hotel, The Santa Catalina. One was 17. I think Peik Larson, the Norwegian young man, had a major crush on Eleanor. The other gentleman was an Englishman named Martin Essex. He was a 27-year-old barrister. We had a lovely time with them investigating the island, playing cards, sitting by the pool and chatting. Peik wanted to come to New York the following summer and visit with us. All this loveliness ended when Eleanor and I had a most unpleasant experience with anti-Semitism via Peik's father, "the commodore," and his mother Balbo. It is quite a long story and you shall have to ask Eleanor to give you the blow by blow of this episode. Suffice it to say, we were at dinner and they, not realizing we were Jewish, made several derogatory comments about some other people in the restaurant who were Jewish.

The final stop of this fabulous trip was Madrid, Spain. Eleanor kept asking me how our next and last hotel could be so very inexpensive. I thought we just lucked out. Our itinerary clearly stated: four star hotel, accommodations: one suite.

Well, when we landed in Madrid, late at night with four large suitcases, a large assortment of smaller luggage and "the crate," the taxi driver asked in Spanish if it was the correct hotel. Eleanor spoke no Spanish, but found someone at the airport who spoke "Spanfrenchis" and he told the taxi driver, "Si, este hotel es correcto." All the luggage was packed into the small trunk of the taxi with 90 percent of it piled on and tied to the roof. Off we went! Need I tell you the hotel was in a slum of Madrid with streets featuring clothes lines stretched from one tenement across the road to another tenement. We looked at each other and thought our travel agent must have had a mental breakdown. A young boy of about twelve was the porter and he had to make six trips up three flights of stairs to bring the luggage to the suite. But this was the best part: the suite consisted of an entry room of four feet by four feet with a dirty pink satin chair, whose back was in the shape of a heart, and a single light bulb dangling from the ceiling. The remaining room of the suite, our bedroom, made the entry room look like Spain's royal palace. Eleanor remarked, "What a horror this place is." I don't think she was overwhelmingly pleased. However, because she was so worried about the young boy carrying all our things down three flights of stairs immediately after carrying them up to "our suite," she acquiesced to spend the night. Eleanor opened one small bag, took out two scarves for our heads, and proceeded to lie down on the bed fully clothed, including her coat and scarf, and asked, "May we leave promptly at seven a.m.?" We did and left the hovel for the world class Ritz. After a long bath and "double shampoo," Eleanor emerged from our enormous marble bathroom in still another stunning outfit. I think she had carried half of Saks Fifth Avenue across the Atlantic. She said, "Let's see all of Madrid; I am so happy and refreshed."

There are two very amusing stories involved with our stay at the Ritz. The first was an incident with a count, who, I was told, came from one of the oldest and most prestigious families in Spain. After spending the day touring, we were ensconced in the magnificent Ritz lobby. We had ordered drinks and suddenly a very young boy in full Ritz livery, (one of a myriad of pages that the Ritz employed) kept walking around with a placard on a gold pole topped with tiny gold bells, announcing, "Senor Ricardo Brrrrrenner." By the third time of the page's circling the lobby, Eleanor said, "It must be you, Rick, that he is calling for." I thought that it was not possible since we knew no one in Madrid and no one knew we were there, but I decided to follow the page to the concierge desk. The head concierge, also in full Ritz livery (only the Spanish had this amazing sense of lavishness and detail to uniforms for their jewel-in-the-crown hotel) presented me with a magnificent, engraved card with the count's crest. In a rather awkward manner, the concierge very politely requested that I follow him. We went to the men's rest lounge which was not only huge but also exquisitely decorated with damask sofas where the concierge presented me to the count. The count bowed and explained to the concierge, who then interpreted for me, that the count wanted the pleasure of my company for a full tour of Madrid tomorrow. His driver, who spoke English (or so the count said), would explain all the buildings and sites to me and then we would dine for lunch at three o'clock at his palace. Not quite knowing what to say, I answered: "I don't think my wife would be very happy left on her own in Madrid." The count gushingly apologized and said, "Of course not. I will have another car and driver at her disposal and the driver will bring her to the best couturier in all of Madrid." I thanked the count and said I would let him know tomorrow morning. I walked back to where Eleanor was sipping her champagne and said, "We have to go to our suite NOW!" She was surprised, but could tell by the urgency in my voice that we were going. When we got to our suite, I told Eleanor the story of the count. She could not stop laughing. I decided to have room service for dinner that evening in our salon, something I generally do not like to do. Anything to avoid the count.

The next morning our doorbell kept ringing. Eleanor pulled on her penoir, raced through the bedroom into the salon, and opened the door. She saw small feet and the most gigantic arrangement of white carnations. Taken aback, she asked the "small feet" to put the arrangement on the coffee table. After he left, Eleanor found the count's card! With great mirth she reentered the bedroom announcing in Spanish R's, "Señor Ricardo the count looks forward to your day together," with that she collapsed on the bed in uncontrollable laughter. We spent the next few days using the service elevator and entrance in and out of the hotel to avoid meeting up with "the count."

RETURNING TO THE U.S.A.

On our last day, before leaving the Ritz late in the afternoon for the airport, I realized that I had quite a few traveler's checks, and we still had the unlimited letter of credit which could still be used if necessary. The problem for me was that I did not want to use any of this, but preferred instead to simply use up our few remaining pesos. I told Eleanor that we would have lunch in the hotel dining room. I said, "They serve wonderful rolls and bread and incredible green olives, all gratis of course." I suggested we order only the famous Ritz onion soup and for the first time on our trip, I felt that we did not need to buy bottled water. "I am sure the hotel tap water at the Ritz is perfectly safe," said I. Well, it wasn't. At the airport I seated Eleanor with the crate (remember the sterling pitcher) and about 20 other items. All of this, I planned to carry on board for our flight. To add insult to injury, I did not do very well with the air service people. They insisted our baggage was extremely overweight and after a full hour of negotiation I still had to pay 200 U.S. dollars! (This would now be at least equivalent to three thousand U.S. dollars.) I returned to where I had left Eleanor and sure enough, there was the crate and assorted items and her purse but no Eleanor. I was flabbergasted and asked someone where the ladies' room was. I was directed towards green beads. This was the curtain and/or the door. The bathroom at the Madrid airport did not have toilets, but rather holes in the ground better known as squat toilets. There was my bride squatting over one of them looking like death and two other ladies screaming at my intrusion. Obviously, Eleanor had dysentery (probably from the tap water at the Ritz). She said, "I cannot leave," and I said she was going to leave, no matter what, because the next plane to New York was not scheduled for three days. I half carried her out of the bathroom and loaded up all our belongings. Without doubt, I was the major Sherpa. Once on board the plane, Eleanor disappeared into the rest room not to reappear for over two hours. I then encouragingly told her, "Darling, you'll feel better in an hour or so." She looked at me and did not say one word. (For those of you who know Eleanor, this is most unusual.) After about another hour, I also came down with "the revenge of Spain" and spent a good part of the remaining 28 hours in the bathroom. Eleanor stayed huddled in her seat with three blankets and two pillows. (The stewards and stewardesses felt very sorry for her.) At one point, after returning once again from the bathroom I moaned and I think groaned. Eleanor leaned over and, in a very soft voice, said, "Darling, you'll feel better in an hour or so." I remember those were the only words she spoke from Madrid to the Azores (we refueled there) to New York. We landed at Idlewild Airport (now known as JFK). Eleanor's mother and father greeted us at the airport. They commented on how poorly we looked after having been away for five weeks. C'est la vie!

1185 PARK AVENUE

Before our honeymoon, Eleanor searched for an apartment and found a four-and-a-half room apartment at 110 East End Avenue (8E). This was across the street from New York's mayor's mansion. We stayed there for about two and a half years, long enough for Eleanor to give birth to our second child, Patricia. We then had to find a bigger apartment and Eleanor networked and found a possibility at 1185 Park Avenue. It was a very grand eight-room apartment that was half a city block in width. We were to share the elevator with one other family, the Fishers. Mrs. Barney Peck, a recent widow, and her son Steven were handling the sale of her cooperative. It was 1959 and I never conceived that I would be able to buy such an elegant apartment. Eleanor held the back of my belt as I tried to leave so I stayed and eventually made an offer that I thought, for sure, they would turn down. The offer was the purchase price of $27,500, a down payment $10,000, and to pay the balance of $17,500 monthly over six years with an interest rate of 2.5% per year. To my utter chagrin and amazement they accepted my offer.

Here we were with a Park Avenue apartment and our next door neighbor being Avery Fisher. Avery was the founder of Fisher Radio Corporation, who subsequently made a huge donation to completely renovate the Philharmonic Hall at Lincoln Center which after it reopened was formally named the Avery Fisher Hall. We had also bought the apartment reasoning that it was in a fine public school district, PS6. We would thus be able to avoid the private school hassle and cost. We were in the apartment less than a year when our side of the street was gerrymandered out of the district, even though across the street, on the west side of Park Avenue and the side streets of 93rd and 94th Streets were included. This was a temporary setback to our plans. Maxine Pines, another neighbor in our building, was to become a very close friend for over 50 years and who played a big part, as you will read, in how our life was to develop.

Tony and Patty on Park Avenue: 1961

Patricia and Anthony: 1963

Tony: 1964

Patty: 1964

Our first child, our son, whom we named Anthony after my mother Agnes, was born September 24th 1957. Our second child, our daughter, whom we named Patricia after my father Phillip, was born March 15th 1959. Tony and Patty spent their pre-kindergarten years at the 92nd Street Y nursery school. I do not really remember the cost per year at that time, but I have recently been told that tuition is now $28,000 per year, per child. I also understand that it is nearly impossible to get a child into the Y without a legacy, an enormous contribution or "top of the line pull," and this is for a three-year-old. Following the 92nd Street Y nursery school, Patty and Tony attended a small private Presbyterian Church school for their elementary education, where there were only 8-12 kids in a class. This was the oldest private co-educational school in the state of New York. Alexander Robertson was wonderful as the small classes allowed for more intensive elementary education and created an excellent foundation for what was to come—and you couldn't beat the cost. It was an outstanding school run by a Scottish Presbyterian minister named Reverend Spence. This was followed by a fine education at The Riverdale Country School, located in Riverdale, New York, about 35 minutes by school bus from 1185 Park Avenue. Riverdale was an excellent private school with a beautiful campus. Both children thrived there and graduated, with Tony going to Yale University and then Stanford Graduate School of Business. Tony graduated Phi Beta Kappa from Yale and was an Arjay Miller Scholar (top 10 percent) at Stanford. Upon graduation from Riverdale, Patty went to the University of Pennsylvania and spent half a year at Princeton. She graduated from the University of Pennsylvania Summa Cum Laude. I must say this was the highest scholarship award in the Brenner family. Patty then attended the Stanford Graduate School of Business and graduated from there with her MBA, as had Tony. Both of our children became enamored with Stanford and the West Coast and ultimately settled in California. Tony went on to a successful career in finance and Patricia achieved acclaim and success in the toy industry. But that will be their story, if they ever choose to write it.

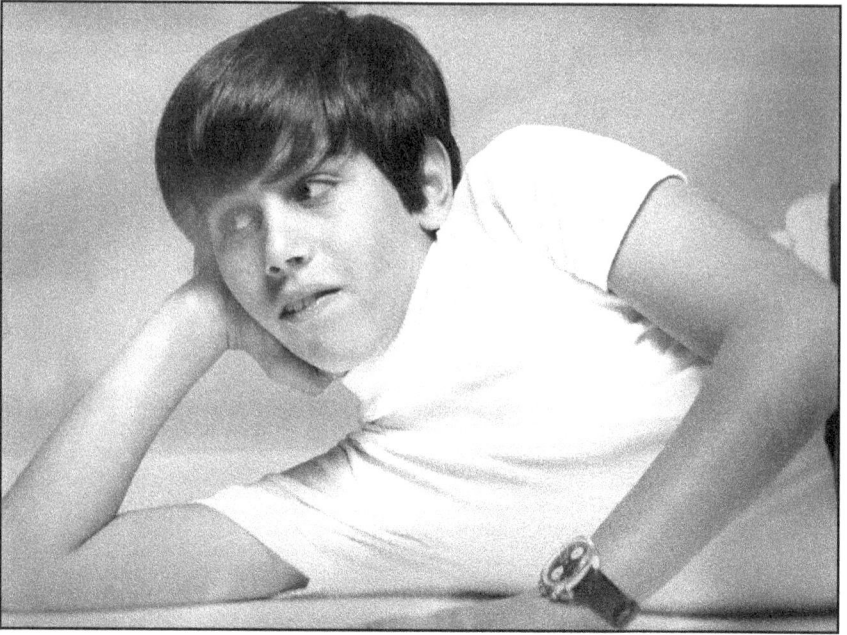

Anthony: 1971

We have four grandsons, Christopher and Jacob in Patricia's family and Alexander and Maxwell in Tony's family. A great sadness to us is that our eldest grandson, Christopher, is severely autistic and could not respond to our family's many endeavors to help him.

After the birth of Patricia, Eleanor came down with a form of Addison's disease. At first, her Addison's was badly handled by an endocrinologist who loaded her with cortisone. After six years of steroids, she developed nephritis, a kidney disease. Through a friend's recommendation, she went to Duke University Hospital under the care of Dr. Walter Kempner. He was the famous originator of the "rice diet" and had achieved remarkable success with it. For many years Eleanor was on a very restricted diet of tiny portions of rice and vegetables with absolutely no salt twice a day. This virtually saved her life, but also necessitated her spending a great deal of time at Duke, which was difficult for all, but thank goodness she completely recovered. We are truly indebted to Dr. Kempner.

Our neighbors for 40 years at 1185 Park Avenue were Janet and Avery Fisher. Shortly after moving in we received a note from Avery explaining that the cooking odors from our kitchen went under our back door, across the service hall, and under his back door and into his apartment. He was very distressed about this and became even more so with time. Our cooking odors became a contentious issue for several years and created a strained relationship. Finally he said he would like to buy and engineer an industrial fan for us but that we must promise to use it every time we cooked. When we would open the window and turn on this fan, all the cooking odors would evaporate. He, the genius of Fisher High Fidelity and founder of Philharmonic Hall at Lincoln Center, precisely measured and built a complete industrial fan enclosure that not only completely took out the odors when the window was open but also created a wind tunnel to the outside. Our housekeeper of many years, Jemima, complained that the vacuum and draft gave her neuralgia and hated the fan. She wore a wool scarf on her head while cooking. It was a no win situation—except for the end of a difficult situation and the beginning of a long friendship.

WHAT COULD HAVE BEEN A GREAT TRAGEDY

When our daughter, Patty, was 12 years old we went looking for a summer home in Far Hills, New Jersey. Since Eleanor and Patty were very involved with horses and loved to ride, we thought this would be a perfect place. We had a frustrating day in finding the right house. On the way home, Patty started complaining of a ringing in her left ear. She said the sound was like a whooshing noise, and also complained of pain in her left ear. We took her to our pediatrician and she was immediately taken to the hospital since she had no hearing in her left ear. She was to stay in the hospital for the next two weeks. We were subsequently to learn that she had been bitten by a mosquito carrying encephalitis. This was the cause of her permanent loss of hearing in that ear. We were very, very fortunate because if the mosquito had bitten her in her head...

Pat is really a remarkable person and overcomes problems and moves forward. Since then she has had to cope with a very severe case of Lyme disease. We are very proud of her and have great admiration for her strength of character and excellent resiliency. You would never know that Patty is not able to hear in one ear. Our daughter is not only a brilliant and remarkable person, but also has a spectacular sense of humor and is a joy to be with.

ELEANOR'S ATELIER

When Eleanor became pregnant with our son Tony she was fired from her TV host daytime show on the New York station Channel 5. No pregnant woman was allowed on TV at that time. Not wanting to waste the remaining four months, typical Eleanor, she enrolled herself in design school in order to learn draping and pattern making so as to be able to design and construct fabulous clothing for herself. This was the height of summer and she commuted to the school by subway even when she was in her ninth month with Tony, taking a cross town bus to the IRT subway at 86th Street and then going downtown by subway. She was an excellent student and had a great flair for design and the comprehension for draping and clothing construction. She continued with design school between her pregnancies and graduated eight months after she gave birth to Patty. Eleanor set up a little atelier on East 52nd Street and had several seamstresses making the clothes for her and friends. One of those friends was Maxine Pines, who worked for Henri Bendel on 57th Street, where she had her own shop at Bendel's. Geraldine Stutz was the president of Henri Bendel. The look and feel of this store was determined by Geraldine Stutz. Bendel's was a very exclusive, forward-looking store that carried expensive merchandise with an avant garde look. One day Geri Stutz stopped Maxine and said how much she liked Maxine's clothes and asked, "Where did you get that stunning outfit?" Maxine told her, and Geri said she would like to see Eleanor's clothes. They met and Geri was very impressed and engaged Eleanor to design, under Eleanor's name, an exclusive collection for Bendel's to be sold in the "Fancy" department, which was their couture department. This was followed by Eleanor selling her clothes to several other fine specialty stores in America, who were always searching for exclusive merchandise. It was a great deal, as these stores did not conflict with her arrangement with Bendel's. I mention this because Eleanor's creative talent played a significant part in what was to happen in our future.

During the 60s, my stepmother was making life very difficult for Eleanor. One day Eleanor called me in tears and told me the problem with Rita. I said to relax, that I would handle the situation. I then called Rita and told her in no uncertain terms that Eleanor was my wife and I expected her to be given the same respect that I was entitled to. From that time on Rita treaded much more carefully, and I realized that in family life one has to seek the same respect as one would from friends and other acquaintances.

Also during the early 60s, I began investing in Dome Petroleum, at that time, a leading Canadian oil company. I built a big position relative to my means and was buying this position on margin. "Margin" means borrowing money against previously purchased stock to buy additional shares, thereby achieving the maximum leverage possible but paying interest on the borrowed funds to the brokerage firm at the going market rate on a daily basis. As an example, if the margin was 100%, you effectively doubled your position as well as doubled your risk. This was fine as long as Dome Petroleum was going up. But when the market crashed, the brokerage company immediately demanded more and more money to maintain the margin of 100%. If you failed to meet the call, they would sell out your account to cover the short fall. The demand was usually for same day coverage of the amount that you were short. This is exactly what happened to me, effectively wiping out all our liquid capital.

It was a great and very painful learning experience and I never again bought on margin. I determined at that time that I would never again be in a position where I could not decide when to buy, hold, or sell a stock, as opposed to giving that decision making authority to a brokerage firm that had to, by law, meet the margin requirements imposed by the stock exchange.

While at Bloomingdale's I received outstanding job offers in California and New York City. Since the people who were eventually hired to fill these positions were to move on to become presidents of their respective stores, I realized what great opportunities they were. However, Eleanor did not want to move to California, since her father had had a serious a heart attack, and wanted to remain on the East Coast. In addition, she was concerned with "the California Style." She felt that Los Angeles had values that were alien to ours. She felt that we would find it ugly and offensive "to keep up with the Jones's." Mostly, she was very concerned that this would be a deterrent to our children's upbringing. We both did not want discussions of how rich someone was, or what they owned, or how important they were… and that was definitely the Los Angeles modus operandi. The New York position had some onerous aspects, so I passed on it as well.

As I look back, I realize life works in mysterious and often wonderful ways. If not for Bloomingdale's, I would have never met my true love or taken the paths that we did.

ROYAL LYNN/REVLON

In 1967, I was approached by Victor Barnett, a former fraternity brother, to become the president of Royal Lynn Incorporated. Royal Lynn was a subsidiary of Revlon that manufactured women's clothing in Hong Kong and sold its products primarily in the United States. Revlon, at that time, was a huge company in the cosmetic field. It had been developed by Charles Revson and his partner. Revson was a very aggressive marketer of cosmetics and backed this up with strong, extensive and dramatic advertising. It was an enormous company with the Revlon brand being sold successfully throughout the world. Charles Revson's reputation was twofold, one being a dictatorial leader and two an obsessive CEO (which I was certainly to witness). At this time I was thinking of leaving Bloomingdale's, and with Eleanor as the designer, starting a dress manufacturing company. I believed that I needed experience in manufacturing and wholesaling and thought that the fit, with Revlon, would enable me to gain such knowledge through Royal Lynn. The company had been run, or maybe I should say mis-run, by the Cole Brothers, Al in New York running the day-to-day operation and Martin in Hong Kong living the "large" life and paying little attention to the factories he was supposed to oversee. The clothes were designed in New York, but the label had never developed a loyal following or significant market penetration. After brief negotiations, I accepted the offer to become president of Royal Lynn.

Charles Revson telephoned me shortly after I joined the company and summoned me to have dinner with him and his wife Lynn (who, incidentally, the company was named for). It was June 19th, which, as many of you know, is my birthday, and this was the only time that I failed to celebrate it with my family and close friends. I remember Revson picking me up in a huge black Rolls Royce that was so tall you just stepped into it without having to bend. It was a pleasant dinner but rather stiff and awkward since he preached his concepts during the entire evening. He mentioned time and again that the most outstanding couture designer, Norman Norell, from whom his wife bought clothes, should be the designer we must emulate. His wife Lynn, a sweet woman, said very little at the restaurant. She wore three huge diamonds pinned like a fraternity pin on her left breast, as well as three beautiful diamond bracelets and a 20-karat diamond ring.

During dinner I suggested that Eleanor, who had developed an excellent couture business and was carried not only by Bendel's in New York City but other fine specialty stores in America, be brought in as a designer to broaden our merchandise appeal at Royal Lynn. Charles Revson indicated he would like to see her designs, but first wanted to have dinner with us at his favorite restaurant, Lafayette. As an aside, when we had dinner with him, he went into the restaurant with his own food, prepared by his own chef, and he instructed them how and when to serve it. At this dinner he again talked about Norman Norell and his theories about color and merchandising. Shortly thereafter, he came to our apartment to see Eleanor's designs. He reviewed the designs and, although he had lots of comments and opinions, was favorably impressed. He offered an excellent compensation package, and Eleanor agreed to join Royal Lynn. However, out of respect and loyalty to Geri Stutz, she simultaneously delivered her couture label to Bendel's that spring while designing for Royal Lynn.

Several months later, Charles decided to sell the company and all non-core Revlon holdings in order to concentrate only on Revlon and its beauty products. Eleanor's employment, and that of her staff, was terminated that day. She was literally tossed out on the street. Shortly thereafter he tried to force me to resign, which I refused to do until we renegotiated my contract and severance pay. I did quite well with this. Since Patty and Tony were in summer camp for three more weeks, Eleanor and I hopped on a plane bound for Lisbon and enjoyed a great holiday.

As an aside, the most important thing in the world to Charles Revson was his business. When he came down with terminal cancer, he divorced his wife Lynn, giving her a great deal of money, probably less than she was entitled to, but making sure she had no ownership or involvement in his true love, Revlon.

Royal Lynn was a good learning experience for me. The company lacked discipline, direction and team work, which are all essential to being successful. Rather, the company was divisive and undermined by conflicting management actions. It was a very negative experience, but one from which I learned a great deal. I came away understanding that a good company should have a pyramid type of philosophy which is determined by the leader at the top and filtered through the organization, being continuously reinforced and emphasized. In addition I resolved that never again would I celebrate my birthday in a business meeting and certainly not without those I love.

CENTRAL SYNAGOGUE

In the 70s and 80s, I was very active in Central Synagogue, our temple in New York City. Central Synagogue was founded in the mid 1850s by an amalgamation of two temples. It is located at Fifty-Fifth Street and Lexington Avenue and is a most beautiful sanctuary created in Moorish style architecture. It is one of the leading reform temples in America and has a very impressive, affluent and prestigious congregation and wonderful rabbinic staff. During my 22-year tenure on the board of trustees, I refused repeatedly to become president of the congregation as I felt I could not dedicate sufficient time to its needs and to the needs of the members. It was very exciting to see the temple grow both in membership and stature. Our son, Tony, was the first Bar Mitzvah that Rabbi Sheldon Zimmerman performed. Shelly was young and very spirited and had just become the assistant rabbi at the time Tony began his Bar Mitzvah preparation. Rabbi Zimmerman worked with Tony and they became very fond of each other. He even went to several of Tony's fencing matches at Riverdale during this period and was very encouraging to him. Within four years he became the senior rabbi at Central Synagogue.

Many years later he left Central Synagogue and joined a huge congregation in Dallas, Texas, as the senior rabbi.

One of the most satisfying experiences for me was to serve on the committee to find a new rabbi to succeed Shelley Zimmerman. The committee was not making very good progress in finding a new rabbi when I suggested that Rabbi Peter Rubenstein be considered for the position. Peter Rubenstein was a senior rabbi at a temple in San Francisco, and I believed he would be an excellent candidate. I had met Peter previously, and I had been very impressed with his presence and pastoral attributes as well as his warmth and intellect. Peter came to New York City for an interview and following rigorous appraisals was offered the position of senior rabbi at Central Synagogue. Today, Rabbi Peter Rubenstein is considered one of the leading reform rabbis in America and has achieved great success speaking from the pulpit of one of the most outstanding reform synagogues in America, Central Synagogue.

FIRST BRENNER DRESS BUSINESS

After Revlon, Eleanor and I decided to go into the dress business ourselves. We studied the potential opportunities and selected the lower end of the more expensive dress market. Neither one of us had experience in production and we thought, at the time, that we needed a production partner. (Boy, were we wrong!) We hired a man as an equal partner to handle production. He had been a production man for many years at other firms, and came with good references. Later we were to realize that the references were not honest or reliable. I always believed after that experience that it is very important to give people who request references reliable and honest answers. I think, currently, many people, fearing a lawsuit, are very hesitant to give a negative reference regarding an executive level person.

The sample collection was designed by Eleanor and shown at the York Hotel at 35th Street and Seventh Avenue. We started out just great and booked immediate business, but there was a major problem: namely, the very obese partner! He was a prima donna, a pervert, and most of all a pathological liar. He padded our production costs and took kick-backs from the contractor and the supplier. After some months I decided I could not allow this to continue. I went to him and said, "You are disgusting, and we do not want to have anything to do with you. Buy, sell or liquidate, it's your choice." Nothing reached him and he refused to make a decision. Finally I padlocked the front door of the factory, and only at that point did he step forward. He offered to buy us out at a very low-ball price which he did not believe I would accept, but I did. Unfortunately, he never paid, and we ultimately closed the business. Incidentally, shortly after this, both of our kids became ill and had to be hospitalized, Pat with salmonella para typhoid and Tony with double pneumonia. This was the only time in our lives without health insurance. There we were, broke, owing a lot of money to our suppliers (whom our partner had never paid), and with two kids in the hospital. We had to take a bank loan to pay for their hospital stays (Tony 10 days and Patricia 16 days).

We went to friends to borrow money to start Brenner Couture. It was not easy to raise, but we started once again in business with $65,000 of borrowed money. This was a very small amount with which to undertake an apparel business. We were so blessed and paid back all investors with interest before the end of our first fiscal year. We were very appreciative of those people who lent us the money to start a risky business. They did not do this as an investment but as a favor with no upside except the interest. Emory and Julia Klineman (parents of a good friend, Bob Klineman) were especially generous and loaned a substantial amount to us. Emory was very excited and took great pleasure in our success, and he would often visit with us in our showroom, giving us advice.

One of the good things to come out of the experience with that miserable ex-partner was that Eleanor explained to the kids that we could not live as we had and that we all had to pull together and be very prudent in what we spent in order to get through this period. We told Patty and Tony that there would be no movies, no pizza, no extras at all. Our children were very supportive and understanding. We expressed great confidence that we would overcome this trial and succeed. Many of our neighborhood vendors helped us, such as the food market on the corner, owned by Sam and Rita Porcelli at Lexington Avenue and Ninety-Third Street, as well as Reverend Spence at the Alexander Robertson School. I shall always be indebted to them for their help. It was, in hindsight, a great lesson for our children that money can roll to you and away from you, and that we all had to pitch in and work together to get through this difficult time, while remaining confident that we could rise again to succeed in the future.

It was in early June of that difficult first financial year in business that Tony decided to make money by opening a lemonade stand on the corner of Park Avenue and 93rd Street. Eleanor and I had told Anthony and Patricia, who was to be his assistant, that we would sponsor his original costs, namely Kool-Aid, paper cups and saltines. Tony was adamant about the saltines, as he felt after two free saltines people would be even thirstier and buy at least two cups of Kool-Aid. They stood out in the hot sun from 10 am to 3 pm. After ten days, Eleanor asked them if they had spent some of their money replenishing their product. Tony said absolutely not. In our kitchen cupboards were sugar, food coloring and saltines. To solve the problem of what to do about paper cups, he had Patty rinse and wipe them so they could be reused. How great! No overhead—only profit! Obviously, Tony and Patty received the message.

Question: What did we do next to make a living? We immediately decided to re-enter the dress business and borrow the capital that we needed, since we were pretty much financially wiped out. We scrounged around to all the people we knew and finally raised the money to go into business. I learned from this experience that the greatest lesson was, first and foremost, to work together to get back up after you fall, and secondarily, not to take references at face value and one can never do enough due diligence.

BRENNER COUTURE, EARLY PERIOD

In 1968, Eleanor and I formed Brenner Couture, Inc. I was determined that we must succeed no matter what the problems. I felt that if I had to pull or push this business through manure, that's what I would do. I said, I can learn to handle production and work with the contractors as well as heading up sales, and Eleanor can handle the fitting of the dresses and, of course, the design. Brenner Couture was an immediate success, which I will now tell you a little about. But, before we go on, let me just say that within one year we totally repaid all our investors their principal and interest. It was a wonderful feeling. On to our big success.

THE BRENNER COUTURE
MOMENTUM YEARS

Our first showroom was at 498 Seventh Avenue (at Thirty-Seventh Street) on the second floor. This was the perfect building for the price and look of the clothes that we were showing and selling. We later moved to the 14th floor in the same building as we prospered and expanded. And 498 Seventh Avenue was very good to us and provided excellent buyer traffic for our collection. We began showing the collection for the fall season of 1968, and Eleanor designed a great line that was very enthusiastically received. Out of the collection came Style #516 which became a very hot style that really put us on the map. We sold thousands of this dress to stores at $31.50 to retail for $55. It became our signature dress and was recognized as such throughout the industry. Style 516 was a soft crepe with a mock turtleneck collar, softly pleated skirt and an empire belt.

The company was organized and staffed originally with me, as the president, handling sales, fabrics and factory production, and with Eleanor doing the designing and the fittings of the dresses on a duplicate model. The duplicate model was a size 8. She was not a size 2, 6-foot tall 105-pound high fashion model, but rather an attractive woman with an average body. This model was a key ingredient because you could not possibly succeed unless your clothes fit perfectly. This was one of the things we concentrated on and we were well acknowledged in the market place for our excellent fit.

For the opening of our company we had a minimum staff, which was all we could afford, with our sales being handled by myself and Judith Block, the wife of my best friend, Bob. Later we added to our staff by bringing in our son's first grade teacher at Alexander Robertson, Norma Wilk, whom we convinced to stop teaching and to join us. I was a great believer in hiring the best potential people and then training them in my way rather than picking people from the marketplace. This led me to eventually hire, as we grew, two sales managers, Hank Sinkle for Brenner Couture, and later, Larry Lefkowitz for Brenner Bees, a knit division we formed several years later.

Hank and Larry stayed with us for many years and after we closed went on to their own personal successes. In addition to Judith in sales, we hired an experienced man-Friday named Jimmy, as a do-everything guy to work directly with me. He would receive fabrics, work with factories, place orders for buttons, pack dresses for shipment, and just about everything else that was needed. I opened the place at 6:45 to 7 am, followed closely by Jimmy. He and I closed up generally at 6:30, but sometimes not until 11 pm because it was the only time we had to pick orders and ship dresses. As we grew, we hired Louie, who became our shipping manager. Louie was a complete loner who liked to work his way, early in the morning or late at night, to pull the customers orders and ship the dresses. He was a take charge guy who was a very reliable, honest, and loyal employee and who always managed to get everything shipped on time even though he did it his way.

We also initially needed a pattern maker. This is a key position since the pattern maker takes the sample dresses and transfers them to a paper pattern which is overlaid on the fabric and from which the fabric is cut for the contractors to make into dresses. We were fortunate to hire a fine pattern maker named Harry. Harry was excellent, but no matter what crisis or problem existed, at 12 pm or 5 pm, he walked out promptly to go to lunch or leave for the evening. To round out the team, over the years we added a production manager, more pattern makers, a fabric and cutting manager, many more sales people, accounting office staff, etc. We added in production and sales all the necessary people to grow the business. Our head bookkeeper was Sylvia, followed by Shirley. Our head pattern maker after Harry left was Frank, who supervised all the pattern makers. When the original pattern maker, Harry, resigned, Eleanor was panicked that we would not find a good replacement. I told her that not only would we find a good pattern maker, but that we would find a better pattern maker than we had. Frank was all of that and he was with us for many years before burning out. He was then replaced by Eileen, who was Chinese and a very talented pattern maker as well. It was a strong organization built for success.

I was like a man possessed, determined that, no matter what, we would overcome and succeed (we had no choice). And no matter what, I never took my eye off the goal. I believed that people were elastic and their performance could be stretched. When challenged to do more they succeeded beyond their expectations and having reached a new level could go on to even greater accomplishments. This was evident at Brenner Couture, where all these people grew exponentially. Examples of this were the two sales managers we hired, Hank Sinkel and Larry Lefkowitz. Their stories were also the stories of the growth of the business and how we tried to find the best potential people who we could train our way.

Hank Sinkel was a wonderful guy who originally worked for JP Stevens as a fabric salesman. He had had polio as a child and had to overcome a withered arm. He in fact had sold a great deal of wool crepe fabric to Brenner Couture, and that's how we got to know him. Eleanor thought he was a great salesman and that he would be a fine sales manager for us, and I agreed. We hired him and he became the sales manager of Brenner Couture. He, in turn, about a year later, introduced me to Larry Lefkowitz, who at the time was the salesman for an oil and gas company. Larry had a great sense of humor and was very personable. I brought Larry in as a salesman and trained and taught him; later he became the sales manager of a division that we subsequently launched, called Brenner

Bees. Brenner Bees was a knit operation, as opposed to Brenner Couture which used prime fabrics like wool crepes, wool jerseys, and silks. Brenner Couture presented dressy merchandise as well as daytime, whereas Brenner Bees was primarily daytime. Hank was a fine salesman and we put together a great team. I cannot emphasize enough that all aspects of our business worked together seamlessly to make it a huge success. The people all grew with the business and went on to have future successes. I was always a believer in focusing on sales and calling all the other aspects of a business as sales supporting. This focused everyone on the importance of sales because without sales "you've got nothing." As to mistakes and closeouts, I learned that the first markdown is the best and to take it steeply enough to move most of the merchandise.

One day after we had first started in business, I received a visit from representatives of the trash-haulers union. The trash-haulers union and garment delivery trucks were controlled by the mob and you had no choice but to work with them if you wanted to get rid of your waste or to receive dresses from the contractor. There was only one company, at that time, that hauled the trash, and no garbage could move out of the garment center in New York City without their approval. I invited them into my office and asked them what I could do for them. They said they had plenty of money and excellent factories to put our work into and wanted to be my partner. I told them I had a wonderful partner, my wife, and I did not want or need another one. End of story.

The other union with a lot of power was the trucking union. This union transported your fabrics to the contractors and returned your finished goods (dresses) to you. One Friday afternoon the truck delivered dresses from the contractor to our receiving room. Of course, being Friday, one of the delivery men had had a few too many drinks. The trucker involved was a small fellow of about six-foot-four who was built like a football linebacker. I was called, since he was in the receiving room brandishing a gun. I went out and confronted him and told him to get the hell out of the place and never to come back, which he did, much to my surprise. (Boy, did I really do that!?)

In dealing with the unions, primarily the ILGWU (International

Ladies Garment Workers Union), one had to be very careful and really know what your goal was and what you were trying to achieve. As an example, when a dress was ready for manufacturing, you needed to determine how much labor was required to produce that garment. Basically, you negotiated with the union representative who came to your office in order to break down the cost and thereby determine the labor cost that you paid on a specific garment. It's really an archaic way of actually determining your markup on that garment. The significant edge you had was that you knew which dresses were the best sellers and that's where you fought the hardest to obtain the best price. By so doing you were able to develop the best possible gross margin, which covered a multitude of problems that might occur.

One of the things that always fascinated me was how amazing it was that a style came out to be a success since there were so many opportunities to go wrong: 1) fabric not right or damaged; 2) the need to sell in large enough quantity to build a cutting ticket (contractors made their money on large cutting tickets and reorders since their shop would become more proficient as the tasks became more familiar); 3) pattern maker errors; 4) marker errors (when the pattern is transferred to flat paper for the cutters to lay on top of the fabric for cutting); 5) cutting errors; 6) mistakes when a new duplicate dress is made from the cut lot and checked by the production department on a duplicate model and against the first duplicate dress; 7) errors in the sewing of the finished garment. This is why I say, with so many hands working on the garment, it is amazing that it comes out right.

We were very fortunate that our first factory was owned and operated by Jack Neugesser and his son Terry, who worked closely with us to solve any problems that might crop up. They made our first dress, Style 516, which was a huge success. We ultimately took over the production of their entire factory and they worked exclusively for us. We were greatly indebted to Jack and Terry because we were very proud that their finished product with our label was consistently very well made.

FIRST MAJOR ADVERTISEMENT

Our first major ad was a page in the New York Times with Bonwit Teller in New York City, a famous Fifth Avenue store. Our buyer was Caroline Swearingen, who introduced us to Mildred Custin, who was then the president of Bonwit Teller. Mildred Custin, a visionary, had a great reputation as a fine fashion merchant and started many new fashion trends. She was tremendously impressed with our clothes and gave us a page ad in the New York Times without requiring us to participate in the cost, which was very unusual. Bonwit Teller then coordinated all the Fifth Avenue windows exhibiting our clothes. Bonwit's was at Fifth Avenue between 56th and 57th Street next to Tiffany. There was no better location for any New York store. The ad was beautiful and the windows were just great and we had a grand success. It was planned that Eleanor would make personal appearances at Bonwit Teller Fifth Avenue and all their major branches around the country. Eleanor was great with the customers and the sales people and would sell a great deal of merchandise as well as teach the sales people about the niche market where Brenner Couture belonged. The personal appearance approach was to become a great tool for building our business, and Eleanor trained our sales people to be able to make personal appearances themselves. As an example, we would enter a new season and have a massive schedule of personal appearances (PA's) blocked out for our major customers. We were on the high fashion map. I remember on our way home from a party stopping to view our first Bonwit Teller windows on the evening they were first shown. Our friends, and Eleanor and I opened a bottle of champagne in front of Bonwit Teller and toasted the fabulous windows featuring our collection. We were so thrilled and excited to see our clothes displayed on Fifth Avenue.

This was followed closely by Saks Fifth Avenue. Anne Maddox was our buyer at the time and she loved our clothes and placed them in all the Saks stores around the country. Anne also organized seasonal page ads in the New York Times as well as personal appearances.

Montaldos, with Manny Rizoulis as President, followed this same approach, as did Nieman Marcus. Manny and his wife Katherine were to become very close personal friends. It was all too exciting and thrilling. During the different seasons of our collections, I would send out our sales people and Eleanor to cover all the requests we had for trunk shows and personal appearances. I overdid it one time: Eleanor was sent "on the road" for nineteen days straight during which time she appeared in seventeen stores. We were accepted as a major vender for the leading fashion stores in America.

Our first Christmas Eve, at about 6 pm, we were closing up for the holiday and the phone rang. We debated whether to answer. Finally I took the telephone and it was B. Altman's phoning in a reorder of Style 516 of 40 pieces. What a nice Christmas present!

As an aside, we had an experience in New Orleans, where we agreed to have Eleanor do a personal appearance at Godchaux, a renowned specialty store, which would also include a huge charity fashion show featuring our clothes. We decided we would both go to New Orleans and I would meet Eleanor at the famous Brennan's Restaurant with our respective sales people who were in town for the show. The five of us had a wonderful dinner. Eleanor's plane was late and she arrived just in time for dessert after not having eaten all day. The Maitre d' suggested she have Brennan's famous Café Diablo. She smiled and agreed. Eleanor had been delayed since she was being honored by New York University, her alma mater, and was to receive an honorary doctorate degree in business. After the ceremony she immediately left for the plane to New Orleans. Fast forward: when she finished her two and a half Café Diablos she felt no pain. (For your information, Café Diablo is composed of brandy, triple sec, Grand Marnier, a splash of Benedictine, and espresso, topped with lightly whipped heavy cream.) We all decided to walk to Bourbon Street in the French Quarter to hear New Orleans Jazz. The music was great and the drinks flowed. After our third and final bar, which was Al Hirt's, we started our walk along Bourbon Street to the Hotel du Ville, where we were staying. Eleanor was laughing, happy and high and then, very casually, said to me, "I lost my satchel on the street. You know, Dick, it has a lot of my diamond jewelry in it." I turned around and went running back to look for the bag not thinking we would ever recover it, and two blocks back on Bourbon Street, there it was, sitting in the middle of the sidewalk. Somebody up there was really looking after us!

This was a heady period for us; we worked hard and played hard. I remember when we hit one million dollars in shipments how thrilled and excited we were. It was a time of outstanding financial income as well as psychic income. One day I was catching a plane to go to our Dallas office to sell clothes at the Trammel Crow Dallas Merchandise Mart. The mart was huge and booked a great deal of business, since buyers and stores from the Southwest did not have to fly to New York City with all its tensions, high costs, and plane fares, but could come for two or three days to do their buying in a quiet, easy and relaxed manner. On my way to the airport I was thinking about how much responsibility we had to all the people who worked for us, not only our suppliers but also the hundreds of employees in the factories, who also worked for us. The responsibility was eye-opening and challenging to me.

WASHINGTON D.C. CONNECTION

Eleanor, who is a multi-task talent, set up a relationship in Washington D.C. through the event planning firm of Gretchen Poston and the lobbying firm of Ann Wexler and Nancy Reynolds. This led to Eleanor's selling clothes to a large number of Washington politicos' wives and our developing warm friendships with many of them. Joan Mondale was part of this group. She became the "second lady" when her husband, Walter (Fritz) Mondale, became Vice President of the United States under Jimmy Carter. In fact, Eleanor designed Joan Mondale's inauguration wardrobe and she never looked better. The press Eleanor received was great. She even helped Joan dress for the inauguration, and we rode along with Joan and Fritz to the inauguration in the Vice President's limousine with sirens blasting and a huge motorcycle escort. The inauguration was very exciting and thrilling to attend.

We were to attend several parties at the White House as the Carters' guests, the first being a state dinner a few months after the inauguration. The state dinner at the White House was in honor of President Tito of Yugoslavia. Being in the White House was a thrilling and wonderful experience. You were welcomed to the White House by the U.S. Marine band. Each individual was shown in and announced by a U.S. Marine in full dress uniform including white gloves. It was really elegant. After dinner President Carter introduced Tito to the 100 guests in a short three minute speech. Tito felt he had to respond so he discussed all the existing hot spots in the world in his own language which was then translated into English. This took over one hour and created a secondary problem since the White House had invited several hundred additional people to join the dinner guests for a dessert reception and concert after dinner. They had a long wait!

Richard and Eleanor at the White House: 1978

Over the next four years we dined several times at the Vice President's house, also very impressive, which was called the Admiralty House, since in its early history the Admiral of the Navy lived there. It was an exciting time as Washington opened a new vista of friends for us, such as the Postons, Debbie and John Dingell, Ed Markey and his beautiful and charming wife Joan Blumenthal, one of the stars of NIH (the National Institute of Health). When Joan Mondale came to New York, she generally stayed with us with her Secret Service detail and all. We had been very active in the Democratic Party and worked hard along with Bob Rubin (formerly Goldman-Sachs CEO and treasury secretary under Bill Clinton) to raise early money in New York City for the election campaign of Walter Mondale for President. We attended the Democratic Nominating Convention in San Francisco and were appalled when he took, as his running mate, Geraldine Ferarro. She was not a team player and did not like to campaign after seven in the evening. The convention was crowned with constantly changing announcements and boring speeches, but to be a part of it was an interesting experience. We still see and hear from the Mondales and had dinner with them in Santa Fe in 2008.

DAIMLER-BENZ EXCITEMENT/ ATLANTIC CITY

One year for Eleanor's birthday, the only thing she wanted was a Daimler-Benz limousine. I bought a Daimler limousine with 2,000 miles on it in a private sale. There were only four or five of these beautiful limousines in the entire country. The seats were made of very soft, black leather. The entire dashboard and the wood at the top of the doors and the dining trays for the back seats were made of solid burlwood. (Today, only veneer is used, as burlwood is rare and prohibitively expensive.) Lucky me, I bought it. No one could service this car and wherever we went it would break down and have to be returned to New York City on a flat bed and delivered to a foreign car expert who charged a fortune and never fixed it properly. We later found out that he was totally dishonest and charged us for work he had never done. One summer we took the Daimler to visit our children at camp in Maine and we got part way there when it broke down, yet again! We had to rent a car and then fly to the part of Maine where Tony's and Patty's camps were and then rent another car to get us there from the airport. We repeated this procedure all the way back to New York City. Of course

Eleanor's beautiful Daimler had to be brought back to New York on the flat bed. The same thing happened on the New Jersey turnpike on our way to Atlantic City for a weekend.

One snowy, icy day, the factory had a problem and badly needed a roll of fabric. I said I would take the limousine and bring the fabric to them since all our employees had stayed home due to the snow, which I probably should have done as well. I drove exceptionally slowly to Brooklyn and returned safely to New York City. On 8th Avenue at around 10th Street the road turns, and as I turned I skidded into a big truck that was illegally double parked. I finally told Eleanor either the Daimler was leaving or I was. It was a tough decision for her and I don't think she was totally thrilled with the decision. A young man from Shirley, Long Island, who collected Daimler-Benz cars, bought the car. He was the grandson of the founder of Shirley, Long Island. I felt badly that I was selling him a lemon and that I was taking advantage of him so I told him all the problems we had had with this vehicle. He proceeded to get on the ground and look under the car, after which he opened the hood and examined the work that had been done. After finishing his inspection he said that a new transmission and the other repairs we had paid for had never been done.

After that experience we had three other cars that were a story in themselves. Our first car was a Humber which was an exciting British import. There were very few in the United States, but luckily it ran like a dream. The second was a Mercedes 280. At the time New York City was hit with a rash of car thefts of expensive cars. After the Mercedes was delivered by our garage to our home it was stolen right in front of 1185 Park Avenue, early in the morning. The third car, the Toyota Supra, was stolen a year or so later in front of a club in mid-town Manhattan.

Our lives were exciting and fulfilling. We worked very hard and we played very hard. We had a lot of international friends with whom we traveled and partied. Le Club had opened in the early 60s. It was a private eating, meeting and dancing club and we joined in 1969. It was super fun because a lot of us would always end up there for a late dinner or after a party for dancing.

The true joy in our lives was our two amazing children, Anthony and Patricia. We tried to have dessert with them every night (they had their dinner much earlier than we did, so while we were having our dinner they had their desserts). During this time we would discuss their day's events. (As an aside, every morning while I was shaving Tony would come into my bathroom and put the toilet seat down and sit and tell me everything that was going on in his life.) After dinner, if needed, we helped Tony and Patty with their homework. About two or three nights during the week, we would go out after Patty and Tony were in bed, to a party or for a drink and dancing at Le Club. We devoted Saturday and Sunday to being with them. Eleanor rode horses with Patty every Saturday morning in Central Park. I played tennis with Tony every weekend at least once, and often twice, and we had many hotly contested matches. Saturday afternoons, the kids generally had plans with school mates or sports leagues and Sunday was always family day. Our lives together were rich and full.

ELEANOR'S BROKEN BACK

It was late in the summer of 1971 and we were planning a long weekend on Cape Cod in Provincetown, Massachusetts. Eleanor had left earlier in the week and I was coming up Friday with Norma and Jerry Sitkin on Jerry's plane. Eleanor had met Jerry while recovering from her kidney disease at Duke. Jerry was from Lewisburg, Pennsylvania, where he and his brothers were in the scrap metal business. Jerry unfortunately had lost his leg due to diabetes. All the details had been worked out and I was to leave from Teterborough, a small airport in New York that catered to private planes. Everything went smoothly and as planned. We were scheduled to land a little after noon in Provincetown. When we landed another friend greeted me and told me that Eleanor most probably had broken her spine and that we should drive to the Hyannis Hospital. Eleanor, a very experienced and excellent horse woman, had a freak accident due to a child who did not know how to ride and was not being properly supervised. The child was fine because of Eleanor, but Eleanor's horse bucked and reared due to the very strong and harsh pressure Eleanor had applied to his bit to avoid her horse ramming into the child's horse. The little girl had lost total control of her horse and was sliding off. She most probably would have been trampled by Eleanor's horse.

When I got to the hospital, there was Eleanor on a cot that was causing her to stupidly lie in a curved position on her spine right where the break had occurred. The pain was horrific. It was the end of a summer weekend, no doctors, and no rooms available at the hospital with patients lying in the corridors. After eight hours I finally got her into a room with another woman. The pain persisted and the doctor insisted she remain there for at least ten days. Well, the weekend passed and Eleanor stayed in the hospital and they advised us she did not need to be casted even though she had broken six vertebrae. She would only require a brace, but would have to remain there for the 10 days before she could leave. Unbeknownst to me, the room they had finally put Eleanor into was the section of the hospital that treated alcoholics and people with extreme mental disorders. No wonder there were bars on the windows, no telephones in the patients' rooms, and locks on the outside of the doors. I returned to New York at the end of Labor Day weekend to be with our children who were returning to their schools. Being unable to talk to Eleanor during the next three days, I flew back to Hyannis to see what was going on. She was still in pain and that was when I realized the room she was in certainly was not a regular hospital room. The head nurse was adamant that Eleanor remain in the hospital for the next four days, which would complete the minimum 10 day required hospital stay. I returned to New York that night and flew back to Hyannis in four days to take Eleanor home. During my time in New York I had contacted Dr. Constantine Velis, who was an orthopedic surgeon and a friend of ours. He was on the staff at the Hospital for Special Surgery. He asked me to bring Eleanor to his office immediately upon our return from Hyannis. After being as careful as we could during the flight home we reached his office at about 10pm. He literally turned green after seeing her x-rays and told us that Eleanor had an unstable spine and any sudden motion could sever her spinal cord permanently and she would be crippled for life. He said the rules of the Hospital for Special Surgery precluded taking a patient as an emergency if they had been in a previous accident and had been treated at another facility. He advised us to go home and come back at seven in the morning and not to make any sudden motions that would permanently damage her spinal cord. We moved as though we were on a sheet of ice and got through the night and went to the hospital at seven a.m. There, Dr. Velis rebroke Eleanor's back and fitted her with the first of many cement body casts that ran from her neck to her hips. The body casts were very heavy and were worn by Eleanor for eight months, followed by an additional fiberglass cast, which allowed her to barely move and with great pain. We had a business to run and who was going to design our clothes? Unbelievably, Eleanor took this challenge and most improbably came back to work. She had to be rolled out of the car because of the cast, transported into the building to our show room, and helped by several people, but remarkably overcame this giant problem and designed a good collection. We were so amazed and blessed that she was able to make such a fine recovery. We were very indebted to Dr. Velis for his wisdom and care that brought Eleanor through this serious accident and back to good health. For several years thereafter we would be walking along the street and her left leg would give way and she would be on the pavement, but thankfully this too disappeared. Eleanor's guts, determination and strength was astounding and was an inspiration to me and to all of our employees and friends.

Eleanor felt that the largest and most important growth in women's clothes in the coming two decades was going to be with The Executive Woman. She felt that as more women graduated from college, received masters, LLDs, and doctorate decrees, and became mothers, the most pressing problem for these executive, professional women was going to be time. Actually the lack of time. Over the past 15 years, Eleanor had spoken with thousands of women at personal appearances, symposiums, trunk shows and innumerable panels on fashion. As only Eleanor can say: "I had an epiphany on the future of products and purchasing and helping the executive woman." Well, indeed she did.

In 1979 (several years before Steve Jobs introduced the Macintosh computer), Eleanor envisioned an entirely new business concept that was truly revolutionary and was driven by computer technology. Not just a computer in a store, but a personal computer as well. Eleanor envisioned the following:

- Freestanding "Eleanor P. Brenner for the Executive Woman" stores.
- Totally separate departments or "mini-stores" in the best specialty stores in America, such as Saks Fifth Avenue, Neiman Marcus, Bergdorf Goodman, and Nordstrom.
- For each customer who entered one of these stores and purchased clothing, a computer file would be set up.
- This computer file would instantly exist in every Eleanor P. Brenner store and of course in the Eleanor P. Brenner headquarters.
- In addition, Eleanor felt that it was only a matter of a few years that the personal computer would become an integral part of the executive woman's life.
- At point of original purchase, this woman would be asked to check off and add commentary to her personal lifestyle dossier. This dossier included:

Name: _____ Date of Birth: _____				
	Yes		No	
Married				
Divorced				
Children				
Ages of Children	1-8:	9-15:	16-25:	
Profession				
Own Home				
Rent Home				
Own Apartment				
Rent Apartment				
Own Car				
Travel Preferences	Winter		Summer	
Beaches	Cities		Ski Resorts	
Approximate Dollars Allocated per Vacation	$500		$1,000	
	$1,500		Above	
Length of Time per Vacation	1 week:	10 days:	2 weeks:	
Travel with Companions?				
Travel with Children?				
# of children Ages:	1-8:	9-15:	16-25:	
Would you like to have your makeup personalized?				
Have you any problems obtaining insurance?				
Would you like help with your 401K?				
Would you welcome help with investments?				
Would you like to own your residence?				
Commentary				
(To Be Filled in by Customer Advisor:)				
Size Purchased				
Approximate Height				
Eye Color				
Skin Color				
Hair Color				
Style Preferences:	Conservative Clothing			
	Fashion Conscious			
	Fashion Forward			
	Needs Fashion Guidance			
	Favors Certain Colors			
	Which Colors?			

Eleanor P. Brenner Personal History Client Profile

Why would anyone want to fill out this form? Simple! If you filled out the form, you received a gift certificate for $500 for clothing or accessories at any Eleanor P. Brenner store. (Please remember this was 1979 and $500 then is probably the equivalent of $2,500 now.)

Why did Eleanor want to know this? She felt that with enough executive women, she could have an insurance company, a travel agency, an eyeglass company, a cosmetics company, a shoe company, a real estate company, and an investment company set up separate divisions for these executive women. Of course, a licensing fee from all these companies would be paid to Eleanor P. Brenner Ltd.

If this woman client of Eleanor's could receive constant information on how and what to add to her wardrobe and to address any other needs she might have via a letter, a phone call, a visit to one of the Eleanor P. Brenner stores, or her own PC, it was Eleanor's belief she would build a most needed and successful empire for the executive woman.

Eleanor met with many, many investors while working with IBM to develop the software needed for her new company. I introduced her to venture capitalists on Wall Street. The results were not good. Instead of seeing her as a visionary, which she was, they thought she was crazy. No one she met could grasp the concept that the computer was going to be the single greatest tool for selling, for information, for service, for a changing lifestyle. No one would give her any financing.

Eleanor was extremely disappointed! However, she picked herself up, decided that she would create a successful sportswear business geared toward the executive woman, not contend with the unions in New York City, base the business in Hong Kong and live on two continents. She did just that.

Before proceeding, I recently learned that Tony was worried about our closing Brenner Couture and he asked Bob Block if I had enough money. Bob's answer to him was, "If your father knows one thing, it's how to make money, and I would not worry about him."

I went on to several interesting situations which I shall now tell you about.

Eleanor and Patricia: Thanksgiving, 1985

PARIS COLLECTIONS

In 1980 I was approached by Brenda Ruello, a senior partner at Heidrick and Struggles. Heidrick and Struggles was a search firm that major corporations used to identify and hire top-notch senior executives, presidents and chief executive officers. Heidrick and Struggles had a sterling reputation. They did a very detailed analysis of the position they were engaged to fill and determined criteria for that position. After determining the criteria, they did a search for available candidates, interviewed and performed due diligence on the respective candidates, and finally proceeded to make their recommendation to their client, who then made the final decision.

The position they recruited me for was President of Paris Collections America. This included the ready-to-wear lines of two French designers (Yves St. Laurent and Chanel) and one Italian designer (Valentino). Ready-to-wear was much lower priced than the French and Italian couture collections that were sold in Paris, Milan and Rome. The French Director Generale of Mendes, Paris, which owned Paris Collections America, felt that their company and other couturiers had a great opportunity to greatly increase volume and to create substantial profit for their parent companies. Often the couture merchandise and their respective atelier were generally extremely unprofitable and the designer/companies looked to licensees for royalty income. A licensee would license a particular segment in which his company had its own market position and know-how and basically add a business to his company by having a new label and the new designs. As an example, St. Laurent had a substantial number of licensees, such as perfumes, accessories and shoes, as well as jeans made under the label of St. Laurent, and priced for big retail distribution with a substantial royalty paid by the licensee based on net sales. So you can visualize how important these licensees were to the couture houses, often being the only funds that supported their couture.

The focus of the Heidrick and Struggles search was to find someone experienced with apparel who would also be able to develop an additional business for St. Laurent in a lower priced sportswear operation which would be solely owned by Paris Collections. With my experience in retail at Bloomingdale's and in better apparel and my success as a manufacturer at Brenner Couture, they thought I had the perfect background for this position. Heidrick and Struggles strongly recommended me. I met with the Director Generale and he was favorably impressed; shortly thereafter I signed the contract to become president of Paris Collections America.

The experience was very enlightening. There was a strong dislike for Americans among this French group, which I had never suspected or realized. It was not overt, but it was definitely there. Everything I did was reported that very same day to Paris and certainly not in a complimentary manner. The first thing I tackled after I discovered close to a million dollars of St. Laurent old inventory in warehouses around the city was how to get rid of it. Shockingly they had never taken any markdowns or put the clothes on sale to clear out this old merchandise. It was a no-brainer to run a big clearance sale and convert this dead money into dollars. I announced the sale to employees and by the next morning Paris was calling in an uproar, as was St. Laurent's public relations lady, Marina Schiano, in New York City. They screamed over the transatlantic phone call, "St. Laurent does not have sales of any kind!" After much back and forth discussion and frustration they finally understood the need to turn their dead money into dollars and finally, finally they agreed. These sales are now a regular occurrence two to three times a year, every year with St. Laurent, Chanel, and Valentino.

The next major problem was that the St. Laurent sales manager, Patrick Canivet, a real charmer, came to work at eleven, went to lunch at one, returned to the office at three and left work at five, and was never going to change his ways. I placed all the people on a normal work day, and this created another furor and untold complaints to the president of Paris Collections in France, but it went into effect. The most major and serious assignment was my mandate to develop a sportswear operation for St. Laurent. I believed the potential business for St. Laurent in a moderate to better-priced sportswear category was huge. I hired key people for this company: designers, a production staff, a sales manager and several others. When Carl Rosen at Puritan heard about St. Laurent setting up a sportswear business, he had a temper tantrum. He threatened to terminate his huge jean license and to take whatever legal action was necessary to keep St. Laurent from having its own sportswear division. Paris Collection France caved in and terminated the operation. I was greatly embarrassed and had to terminate the people I had hired for the St. Laurent sportswear operation.

In addition to St. Laurent, Valentino incorporated his ready-to-wear, taking it back to Italy where it would be sold solely by Valentino, and decided that the Valentino stores would no longer be part of Paris Collection America. Simultaneously, Chanel announced that they were planning to incorporate their ready-to-wear back into the parent company and open a big show room on 57th Street. This was a time, as you can see, when these companies all wanted to consolidate their businesses under the parent company and they all moved in the same direction at the same time. This, they believed, allowed them to have total control of the design concept, manufacturing, and distribution and to be able to more closely coordinate all these different aspects.

When all that had happened, I was left no choice but to resign and negotiate a settlement of my contract. I had only been there six months, but it was a really interesting experience. St. Laurent sportswear could have been a great success. C'est la vie.

D.H. BLAIR

After leaving Paris Collection America in 1980, I was again faced with the question of what to do next. I was 53 years old and had no intention of retiring at that time. A friend of mine, Harold Wit, introduced me to J. Morton Davis, the owner and CEO of D.H. Blair & Company, Inc. Morty Davis was a classmate of Harold's at Harvard Business School. I met with Morty Davis and learned my first lesson with him. He was always late. Our appointment was for 4pm, but we started over two hours late. (In the future I would call him on the telephone instead of going to see him and thus avoid waiting.) Davis was impressed with me and immediately offered me the position of a managing director at D.H. Blair. There was to be no salary, but a substantial percentage on the business I brought in and developed. Having confidence in myself, this was a fine and fair arrangement.

D.H. Blair was a company at that time which primarily underwrote young companies or took early start-up companies public. I called it Public Venture Capital because it provided young companies with the money they desperately needed to grow their businesses. The company issued stock for an initial public offering (IPO) in which the underwriter, which in this instance was D.H. Blair, would underwrite the subject company, guaranteeing the sale of those shares to the public. A prospectus would be prepared, providing a detailed history of the company, its management, and all pertinent financial information necessary for public investors to make a determination to buy or not to buy the respective stock. The prospectus was prepared by the company's principals, lawyers, and accountants in tandem with D.H. Blair's investment bankers and lawyers. The completed prospectus was sent to the Securities and Exchange Commission (SEC), which reviewed it thoroughly and then sent it back with comments. The prospectus was then corrected by the company and all the lawyers and the investment bankers from D.H. Blair and resubmitted to the SEC until it finally came back with no further comments. No comment did not mean they blessed the prospectus but rather that it was a clear document for the investor to evaluate. At that point the underwriter, D.H. Blair, determined the size, price and timing of the offering, e.g. 500,000 shares at a price of $10 per share to be listed and officially sold to the public on such-and-such a date.

D.H. Blair was responsible for placing the offering whether, it be through its own clients or through the open market (Wall Street) or, usually, a combination of both. This is a great responsibility for the underwriter, and the ramifications can be huge: big profits or, if mistakes are made, big losses. I learned that you can never do enough due diligence on the prospective company. Entrepreneurs and all types of people are attracted to money like a bee is to honey. Therefore, you are approached with hundreds of potential business plans (always glowing) and you must select among them as carefully as humanly possible. One bad deal can hurt you out of all proportion to the many good deals you do. D.H. Blair was also a full line brokerage firm and accordingly had brokers who were hungry for products to sell. Blair was very entrepreneurial and did work in merger and acquisitions as well as private placements and venture capital. It also made direct investments into companies other than through public offerings, usually for a stock ownership percentage. Investments in the private companies could be done in-house or from the outside or a combination of both.

I started on a Monday and was given a desk, chair and phone. No one talked to me. It was as though I was not there. I did not realize when I joined D.H. Blair that it was much smaller than I had thought. Morty Davis was a very interesting character: brilliant, gutsy, and decisive, with a prodigious memory as well as being personable and charismatic. He had had a strict orthodox Jewish upbringing. His complex way of analyzing issues was probably fostered in the Yeshivas of his grade school and high school years. Being an orthodox Jew, he had four daughters. They have given birth to 30 grandchildren and 14 great-grandchildren and are all still living together in a compound in Lawrence, Long Island. Morty was also a great second-guesser. When things went right he always said, "This is a joint venture." When things went wrong he always said, "You are responsible." But, in fact, that goes with the territory on Wall Street. He was 20 years ahead of the "claw back" concept discussed today in the recession of 2008 to 2010. A claw back penalizes investment bankers for failures by requiring them to give back substantial compensation that had previously been realized.

This was the beginning of a ten-year relationship that I had with D.H. Blair and Morty Davis throughout the 80s, which I shall now tell you about.

SOME DEALS DONE AT D.H. BLAIR

Enzo Biochem/Johnson & Johnson

One day shortly after I began, Morty Davis walked into my office and said he had a project for me. A year before I joined Blair they had completed an IPO for Enzo Biochem (EZO), one of the first genetic companies to go public. In order to support the Enzo stock in the marketplace, Blair had bought back a great number of shares and consequently did not have the capital to move forward as aggressively as Morty desired. He said to me, "If you can do a private placement for Enzo Biochem, you can name your own ticket with me." Well, I had a desk and a phone, but where to begin? I was on my own! No executive assistant and no staff. I quickly determined that I had to first become knowledgeable in genetics and especially learn what Enzo Biochem was seeking to develop. I spent a great deal of time with Enzo Biochem's president and vice presidents. The president was Elazar Rabbani and the vice presidents were Sharam Rabbani and Barry Weiner, who was married to the Rabbanis' sister. A tight family affair. They were Iranians and I liked them very much and we became good friends. They completely opened up to me about their business, and I learned a great deal about genetics.

I decided that the direct approach was best. I created a list of potential companies that could possibly invest, and commenced the frustrating and difficult task of cold-calling. After many turn-downs, I had my first hit with Archer Daniels Midland, a great public company ruled by Dwayne Andreas, the CEO. Andreas was very difficult and egotistical, and his people ceded to whatever he demanded. We set up a meeting and met for several hours, after which he arbitrarily and abruptly stated he had no interest in proceeding. He showed no graciousness or sensitivity, and it was not an encouraging meeting. We all left frustrated and disappointed. The second hit was with Johnson & Johnson's development office, where Wally Steinberg was a senior vice president. The mandate of J&J's development office was to find exciting companies with future potential to be important factors in the health care industry. They found this was a much faster and less expensive way to achieve penetration into new businesses than creating their own research and development company. We set up a meeting with Wally Steinberg. J&J picked up the ball immediately and enthusiastically and sent their scientific people to evaluate Enzo and its technology. After months of evaluation and negotiation, including a meeting at the famous Johnson & Johnson House in New Brunswick, New Jersey (which was a good omen since I had been born and raised there), they declared they were interested in making an investment. The technology J&J was interested in and subsequently invested in was a fundamental breakthrough involving a non-radioactive isotope which could identify and mark a molecule or gene. This technology was to be the basis on which many new drugs were to be developed.

Finally, at about six months from the time of the initial introduction, a contract was signed. J&J invested $22 million initially and followed up years later with $50 million more (from which we did not receive any benefit). This was far and away the biggest deal Blair had ever done. The pay-day for me, included cash and warrants and was great.

Morty was thrilled since the stock price took off after the J&J investment. He was able to profitably sell large amounts of Enzo stock that had been choking D.H. Blair and to expand his IPO operation. The customers were pleased because they made money on their respective stock purchases.

Elan Pharmaceutical

Morty again dropped in to say J&J/Wally Steinberg could be an annuity to me by sending me additional deals which they had seen. A couple of months later, without saying a word to me, Morty hired Wally Steinberg as an investment banker, but before he joined Blair, Wally Steinberg referred to me Elan Pharmaceutical, an Irish company, and I did my first IPO with them on January 19th 1982. Elan was, and still is, a major company in the healthcare field. They developed the patch worn to discourage people from smoking cigarettes. The purpose of the IPO was to finance an expansion of Elan in the United States by opening a new facility in Georgia. We placed 770,000 shares at a price of $4.17, which included a three-for-two split in February 1984. (A three-for-two split means that for every two shares you own on the record date you will receive an additional share and now own three shares.) We raised, in total capital, $4,812,500. The offering was a big success and the stock was placed in very strong hands and showed excellent upside from the original offering price. I was very happy with the outcome, as were all the brokers at D.H. Blair. I think it is important to realize that the Dow Jones averages were at 980—1000 in 1982, and a sizeable deal was over $3 million.

About this time, I decided to take the Series 7 exam, which, when you passed, allowed you to become a registered broker. A registered broker could then be hired by a firm to buy and sell securities to customers. This became a lucrative adjunct to the IPOs I was doing. In order to become registered you had to take the Series 7 test after going to classes and studying the material supplied by the SEC. I completed the requisite course work and took the test. I was just about the oldest person among several hundred attendees. We sat in an old fashioned school chair with an attached small writing board. Everyone finished (all the young people) very quickly and exited while I was still working. This made me a little nervous. When I finally finished, I had trouble standing up because my poor back ached from the strange desk I'd been sitting in for such a long time. I went home, changed clothes, and went for an invigorating run around the Central Park Reservoir. A week later I learned I had passed and could do brokerage as well as investment banking.

I thought I had made another major contribution to D.H. Blair, encouraging Morty Davis to end the cold call operation, which might have grown into a serious nightmare since it might have resulted in violation of turnover and spreads between the sale and purchase of stocks if continued. He followed this suggestion.

In my subsequent years at D.H. Blair, I did approximately 22 major transactions and raised in excess of $125 million (in today's money, well over half a billion dollars). Many of these companies are still in existence and others have been sold or merged with bigger companies. It was a very heady time and I learned that Wall Street attracts all kinds of people, including many who are totally dishonest. Money breeds strange bedfellows. In order to be an investment banker you had to be optimistic and to believe in people and, therefore, were subject to failures and disappointment. Now I will tell you about some of the other outstanding and memorable deals that I did while at D.H. Blair.

BioTechnica International

BioTechnica International was one of the early genetic companies to go public. Because of our success with Enzo Biochem, they came to me. BioTechnica was a Harvard/MIT group that worked on genetics in the agricultural field. They were an exceptionally talented and brilliant group of people. The IPO was on March 28th, 1983, for 880,000 shares at a price of $11.25. We raised capital in the amount $7,700,000. (Note: Stock figures reported and placed in the IPO included the over-allotment option, which generally allows the underwriter to elect to underwrite an additional 10% or so of the number of shares originally offered.) The money was spent wisely by the company and they ended up being bought out by Home Farm, a major company in the agricultural farm field. One of the products they had developed was genetically altered corn, which was resistant to diseases and greatly increased corn production. It also enhanced the size, color and appearance of corn.

Thoretec

Thoretec Labs' IPO was completed on May 27th, 1983. A total of 794,500 shares were sold at $13.75, and we raised total capital of $10,965,625. Thoretec Labs was Dr. Bob Harvey and his group from California. They were working on developing a heart pump to temporarily replace one's own heart while undergoing heart surgery. In 2011, the *Wall Street Journal* ran a laudatory article on Thoretec's new heart pump. Amazingly, the company is still operating in the same field 27 years after I worked on its IPO.

Health Care Service Group

Health Care Service Group (HCSG) was a hugely successful IPO completed on November 22nd, 1983. The company sold 644,000 shares to the public at a split price of $2.78, with a 50% stock dividend in October of 1984 and again in April of 1985. Health Care Service Group's name was a misnomer because the company was in the janitorial and housekeeping service business for nursing homes and small hospitals. It was run by Dan McCartney, who was an inspirational and charismatic leader as well as a hands-on operator. HCSG is still in existence almost 30 years later, and today has a market value of over one billion dollars.

Considerably after the IPO, I became aware of a problem with a major shareholder who was also an employee. This man subsequently resigned from the company, and wanted to sell his stock. I was able to place his stock very profitably with people willing to buy restricted stock. (Restricted stock is stock that must be retained by the respective shareholder for a length of time and is not liquid until that date is reached. It is most often early stock owned by the founders and entrepreneurs. In order to protect the public market, it is restricted in its timing. It can also be activated if the company does a secondary offering and holders of the restricted stock become selling shareholders in the secondary offering.) It worked out beautifully and everyone involved was very happy.

Uniforce International, Inc.

Uniforce International, Inc., was another big success. On March 23rd, 1984, the company sold 570,000 shares to the public at a split price of $4.67, with a 50% stock dividend in 1984, and raised total capital of $4,389,000. The company was a personnel placement company for temporary positions, one of the early pioneers in the temp field. The company was managed by John Fanning who was one of the most outstanding sales promoters I had ever met. The company was merged shortly after going public into a bigger temporary company at an excellent price, resulting in a substantial profit for the shareholders.

American Shared Hospital Services

The founder of American Shared Hospital Services was Ernie Bates, an African-American neurosurgeon from San Francisco with an excellent reputation. I mention his color because there were not many companies headed by African-Americans at that time and I was excited to be doing this offering. When we took American Shared Hospital Services public, Ernie Bates was operating mobile Magnetic Resonance Imaging (MRI) and Cat Scanning (CT) machines in hospitals in Northern California. These hospitals could not afford their own equipment since the machines were very expensive and had to have maximum utilization to be profitable. Nevertheless, the hospitals needed to have these modalities available for their patients, so renting them for scheduled part-time use was a feasible and viable solution. Thus, the name "Shared Hospital Services." On July 3rd, 1984, we raised $4,887,500 for American Shared Hospital Services by selling 977,000 shares to the public at a price of $5.

The company still functions more than 26 years later and was one of the earliest providers of the Gamma Knife, a new neurosurgery technology that they were instrumental in launching. The Gamma Knife was a stereotactic radio surgical instrument that performed noninvasive surgery on brain and body tumors. The Gamma Knife is not a "knife," but a device that delivers a focused beam of cobalt-60 radiation to a brain tumor through a target point in the brain. A specialized helmet is surgically fixed to the skull so the brain tumor will remain unmoving at the gamma-ray target point. This is a highly specialized, heavily shielded device that treats the tumor in one session, leaving surrounding tissues relatively undamaged. It was invented in Sweden in 1967. American Shared Hospital Services were very early in the introduction of this technology and offered it to their client hospitals on the same mobile arrangement. The company had a strong board of directors, including two well-known San Franciscans. The first was Willy Barnes, who was the first black Securities and Exchange Commissioner of the State of California. The second was Willy Brown, the politico. Willy Brown, at the time, was Speaker of the House of the State of California and later was Mayor of San Francisco. As an aside, I was visiting American Shared doing due diligence when Willy Brown was giving one of his famous block parties. He took over the entire San Francisco waterfront and the party went from one waterfront building to the next and on and on. There must have been thousands and thousands of guests and almost uncountable bars and food stations. It was quite a party!

While our son, Tony, was attending Stanford Graduate School of Business for his last year, he took very ill and knew no doctor to call. Finally, he was so sick that he did not have the strength to go out. I called Ernie Bates who took over and he had Dr. Mary McDermott call Tony. She arranged to meet him at California Pacific Medical Center, and took him to the emergency room where they performed a chest x-ray. Tony was diagnosed with pneumonia. She put him in the hospital where he finally recovered (except for an allergic reaction two weeks later to penicillin). I always say that you are a parent until they put you in the box.

We took several companies public in 1982 and 1983 in the computer industry. Unfortunately, there was a major a shakeout in this industry at the end of 1983 and into 1984. Some of these companies were sadly involved in those industry problems and failed.

Another aspect of my work at D.H. Blair was private placements and mergers and acquisitions. During this time I did several mergers and acquisitions, one of which was a buyout of Oakley Sport Sunglasses, which catered to the action sports market, i.e. skiing, sky diving, skating, etc. The buyer was a large Italian sunglass company named Safilo. I represented both sides in this transaction and received a fee from each (this rarely happens, but in fact I did bring both sides of the transaction together). I will go on with one more transaction at D.H. Blair.

I had previously worked with the Donzi Boat Company, a high performance motor boat manufacturer. Bill Hall was hired by Donzi to assist the company in raising capitol and brought Donzi to me for a potential public offering. When I went to visit the company in Bradenton, FL, they took me for a ride in their high performance motor boat. It went so fast that it bounced from wave to wave. My teeth really rattled and I was very ready to get back safely to land. Donzi was also building a small trial yacht. It was a beauty. I walked through the yacht and was very impressed.

When I studied the business plan, I became very concerned and promptly called the Donzi folks in for a meeting. Bill came to see me the next day with one of the principals of the company. I told them that not only could they not go public but they were very close to failure and bankruptcy, since they had inadequate capital to meet their current needs and had inadequate management. In addition, I told them they needed to immediately focus on what I believed was a crisis situation for them. I then proceeded to show them where the problem existed. They thanked me profusely and much to my amazement sent me a sizeable fee for the service rendered. Never again was this to happen, and I mention it because Bill had created a great deal of goodwill by so doing.

Learning Experiences from IPOs:

1. The three most important things in an IPO/underwriting are due diligence, due diligence and due diligence.
2. Be sure you fully understand the technology of the respective business because if you cannot understand it, the customer buying the stock won't either.

3. Research and study management as thoroughly as possible because they are the people who make the company work. Determine their past successes and failures and analyze their strengths and weaknesses. The leadership they provide will determine the success or failure of the company. Question whether or not they are flexible enough to modify a concept and even, if necessary, change the direction of the company.

4. Study the future possibilities for the company objectively and thoroughly, including the competitive situation.

5. Study the board of directors and make sure that the public is represented by knowledgeable, independent directors, with people experienced in that area and/or sound business people. A good board can make major contributions to a company's success.

6. Do not do deals with government involvement. They are often unreliable, difficult to get timely answers from, and subject to re-elections and change in policy.

7. Be very careful when a company customizes its product to the needs of individual customers. This often causes costs to become totally out of line and dramatically affects the company's profits.

8. Be careful because many new companies often want the money for acquisitions that are ill-timed and rushed through before they have thoroughly evaluated the target company. Also, many have not properly analyzed and prepared for the use of proceeds from the offering.

In the late eighties, the business began to change and there was not as much opportunity for IPOs. It had greatly diminished with the Tech Bust of 1983 and 1984 and the market crash of October 1987. In addition, there was a sea-change negatively affecting the entire market for raising capital via IPO's for small companies or start-ups. D.H. Blair had been a grand experience, and I enjoyed it tremendously. It was both exciting and very lucrative. But, with the business becoming more difficult, I thought it was time to move on. Morty Davis was very gracious when, in 1990, I told him I was leaving. He said, "Dick, you are always welcome to return to D.H. Blair." It was a very nice parting.

LEVERAGED BUYOUT TIMES

After leaving D.H. Blair in 1990, I worked with a younger associate, Andrew Johns, in the leveraged buyout area. A "leveraged buyout" means you attempt to buy a business using the assets and cash flow to leverage the company, often times working with management as your partner. You must have the bank financing to consummate a buyout, but the key to the deal is that you must have the cash flow to cover the interest as well as to fund the operation. We worked on two deals that we had put together. The first LBO was with a good-sized company that was located on Long Island. It provided aluminum siding for a local neighbor, Grumman Aircraft, a major defense contractor. This deal had an added complexity since we were having the owner sell the business to his employees through an Employee Stock Option Plan (ESOP) as well as to Brenner and Johns. We had negotiated a purchase price with the employees' representatives and everything was finally in place, but when we went to close the deal the owner said he could not sell the business because he was too emotionally involved and would be lost without it. We were frustrated and very upset but the deal was dead. The employees of the company were also very upset, not to mention all of the expenses and time lost which could never be recovered. An after-shock in this deal was the fact that six months later Grumman announced a surprise consolidation and closing of their longtime Long Island facility. The community was shocked but could not convince them to stay. Because the new location was miles away and aluminum siding is heavy and costly to ship, Grumman probably would have stopped buying from our company and we would have been in very difficult straits. Sometimes the best deals are those that are taken out of our hands and not done.

The other LBO that Andy Johns and I worked on was a company that made cockpit controls for Boeing Aircraft. This was another very interesting company with a specialized niche market. Boeing is the biggest United States aircraft maker and enjoys a fine reputation and occupies a dominant position in the industry. Here too we ran into the same problem, where after securing financing and putting all the elements in place for the buyout the owner decided not to sell. It was discouraging, but we did consummate one deal and that one became a problem.

Bill Hall, whom I described earlier in connection with the Donzi Boat Company, was the person who had brought the high performance motor boat company to me, and now he came to me with a new company. Medco Containment was a huge company organized to control the cost of drugs in the healthcare field and to deliver and fulfill the delivery of drugs, passing on savings from bulk purchases. The company was very successful. It was a major acquisition for Merck Inc., which Merck ran for many years before spinning it off as a separate company. Bill came to us with a similar idea of taking control of Nationwide Prescription Services, a small drugstore company located on Long Island. We visited the facility and it was very presentable and looked like it could be converted to a business similar to Medco, but of course much smaller. We worked hard to put together a very strong investment group that would be able to assist in growing the business. The group included Andy Johns and myself but also, and more importantly, a benefit man who was well established on the East Coast. (Benefits programs cover the compensation that employees receive in addition to their salary, i.e. healthcare, insurance, etc.) The benefit man had many contacts with corporations, unions, and institutions on the East Coast and thought he could bring some of them into our program. The other key investor was a prominent labor lawyer from the Midwest who believed that he could bring in union business from the Midwest. Bill was very excited about the business and thought it had great opportunity for success. Bill indicated that he would like to be president and after much discussion we all agreed. We needed to analyze the problems that might occur before we brought in new prospective customers. So we took over the operation of the "drug" store to have a shake-out before we tackled the next step of bringing in major clients. The first audit came through about six months later and we were shockingly out of money. This did not seem possible as we thought we had adequate capital to see us through this early period. We dug deeply into all the costs and finally uncovered what had happened. A key employee had not told us he was going through a very costly and difficult divorce. He finally admitted taking the money that was set aside for the capital of the business to help defer his divorce costs. The investors were shocked, but all had careers and positions that they would not give up to help run the company. So, there we were, with no capital and no management and only a shell of a company. We decided not to prosecute and to write the losses off as a bad investment.

BRENNER SECURITIES

Beginning in 1993, I spent a short period of time at a specialty brokerage operation called Burnham and Company. John Burnham was a very fine and decent man, and I liked him a great deal. I stayed at Burnham and Company until my brother Howard opened a boutique brokerage firm called Brenner Securities. Howard had been at Drexel Burnham for many years and ultimately became president just months before it was pushed into bankruptcy. Drexel Burnham was Michael Milken's firm, and had been founded by John Burnham's father, also a very fine man. Milken originated the junk bond market that funded a great deal of the merger and acquisition business of that day. Unfortunately, the Drexel firm was arrogant and aggressive and stepped on a lot of toes. Other firms on Wall Street, smelling an opportunity to grab this business, did not support Drexel or come to its aid when the company got into trouble. It was a shame, because Drexel Burnham had many outstanding people and very substantial assets and the shareholders ultimately received significant equity from the dissolution of the company. My brother Howard asked me to become a managing director of the new firm he was forming called "Brenner Securities," and this led to the most successful deal of my career.

PENN NATIONAL GAMING, INC.

At Brenner Securities I did the most successful deal I had ever done and certainly the most successful Brenner Securities was to do. In point of fact, it has been one of the best deals done on Wall Street. It was the IPO for Penn National Gaming, Inc., a small company from the Harrisburg, PA area. The deal came to me through my son Tony, who had met and became very friendly with Peter Carlino, the president of Penn National Gaming. Peter and Tony were members of an organization called the Young Presidents Organization, YPO, which was exactly what the name implies. The purpose of the organization was to provide a vehicle for young corporate presidents to share problems with each other as well as to open new horizons and visions to the membership. It is an international organization structured as independent local chapters with over 5,000 members worldwide. Peter told Tony he was interested in doing an IPO and Tony said you should speak to my father, Dick Brenner, who has completed many IPOs and is very experienced in that field. I then flew to Harrisburg and met Peter Carlino and discussed his operation.

Peter Carlino was a builder and contractor for large buildings in the Harrisburg area. He was very shrewd, smart and charming. He was also very driven and aggressive and had a big vision of where he could take his company. He ultimately accomplished even more than he, at that time, had envisioned. But let me not get ahead of the story. I met his people, visited several of his locations and undertook a thorough review of his business plan. He had top lawyers, accountants and backup and was obviously a demanding and performance-driven leader. The business, at the time we took it public, was involved in two off-track wagering locations and one race track in Harrisburg, PA that had a simulcast operation. A simulcast operation appears as a real time broadcast but emanates from a different location. Penn National off-track facilities, through simulcasting, were able to broadcast major races from the bigger and more famous tracks, attracting more customers and achieving greater revenues and profitability than they could have achieved on their own. It is usual for simulcast operations to have a big screen that projects the race and excitement of the moment so customers can bet accordingly. It's the next best thing to being in actual attendance, but without all the hassle of going to the track, and also allows one to bet on races all over the country. Peter's vision was to grow this small off-track wagering operation into a major gaming company, and that's exactly what he has accomplished. It's really quite remarkable.

Because of the size of the offering and the limited stock placement capacity of Brenner Securities, we had to bring in a partner. "Placement ability" means the ability to interest both in-house and outside brokers to distribute and sell the stock at the offering price. "Handling the book" refers to this. I searched for the right partners who would run the book, and we settled on Fahnestock, a medium size brokerage firm. The IPO took place on May 26th 1994 and raised capital in the amount of $18,000,000 by selling 1,800,000 shares at a price of $10. The company sold 1.5 million shares and selling shareholders sold 300,000 shares and respectively netted $13,900,000 and $2,790,000. Next is a chart comparing the company then and now, sixteen years later.

	May 1994	**December 2010**
Gross Revenue	$46 Million	$2.43 Billion
Off Track Wager	2 facilities (Reading & Harrisburg, PA)	19 facilities in 15 jurisdictions *see location of facilities and timeline (attached)
Employees	278 full time / 286 part time & 74 season = 638	14,693 total employees
Stock Price	$10	Stock price $30.25 as of September 9, 2010*

* Cost with splits included is $0.83 per share. This would represent an approximate increase of 35 times original investment share price on a split-adjusted basis. All figures are approximate.

Penn National Gaming

The above figures are approximate and are from various Penn National Gaming Company reports.

I was on my office phone talking to Boston when I heard a loud and very strong explosion. I said to the person that I was talking to that it sounded like a bomb exploding, and seconds later the building rocked from one side to the other from the force of the explosion. Terminating the call, I looked out the window from the 38th floor as all the power and electric on our floor went dead.

About an hour before the bomb went off, I had driven my brother's car into the underground parking and I was to later learn that I had parked it not more than 30 to 40 yards from where the bomb exploded. Fate was so kind to me.

It was a difficult decision to make, but I said to all the employees that we would stay on the 38th floor and wait for rescue. This changed, 30 minutes later, when smoke began to fill the 38th floor, and I decided that it was time to go. Most of the higher landings were dark with all the lights out, so we walked down with your hand on the person in front of you so you could manage the curves on each floor. People were wonderful and relatively calm as we walked down from the higher floors not knowing what to expect at the bottom.

When we finally reached emergency lights it was about the 12th floor and as we exited the building police told us to move quickly away from there in case the building would collapse. I proceeded to call Eleanor to tell her I was OK but she had not heard the news of the bombing. Brenner Securities never did return to those offices but moved up town. It was quite an awful experience but nothing like the disaster of 9/11.

TONY'S QUESTIONS

I have been asked by Tony many times how I was able to have such a varied business career. I never really thought about it until now, but I will try to frame up an answer.

I guess the first answer would be that I never thought I could not learn something new and thus was not inhibited or afraid and would constantly push ahead. I was blessed with great energy, determination, and drive along with confidence in myself. I also have a very supportive wife, who was always there for me in the most positive way.

The last factor was that I had no choice but to push ahead because there was no mentor or rich family member who would be there to support or help me. What I was to accomplish I did the old fashioned way—"I earned it!"

The second question was how we were able to raise two such wonderful and successful children, while many others have raised kids who have floundered.

I think my first answer would be that we were only like coaches. We can take credit for Patricia and Anthony, but they are who they are because of themselves.

However, we did provide great love and tried to make Tony and Patty as self-confident as possible. This love and affection were coupled with limits and discipline on behavior. In addition, the time we spent with our children was quality time. We were not there half-heartedly, but rather completely focused on them.

The last thing is genes.

MEMORABLE EVENTS

Tony's Bar Mitzvah – 1970, September

Tony did us proud. He read the prayers and his portion of the Torah and Haftorah beautifully. His speech, "Why it is so necessary for all Jews to support the United Jewish Appeal," was wonderful. Everyone attending, including our guests and members of Central Synagogue's congregation, were overwhelmed by both the content of his speech and his poised delivery. (Eleanor and I were also shocked and amazed when we heard his speech for the first time that day.) Tony never faltered or missed a beat. Eleanor's mother and father were overcome with pride and joy, and Patty said, "My brother is the best."

Eleanor and I, as previously discussed, had entered the dress business in 1968 and were beginning to gain a great deal of momentum by the time of Tony's Bar Mitzvah in 1970. (This was after our fiasco with the bad partner, which caused us to have to start over.) We wanted to do something wonderful and memorable for the Bar Mitzvah party but did not want to do an extravagant spectacle with no budget limits, as many people were doing. We decided to have a luncheon party for children and adults. Eleanor had fallen in love with the magnificent views and total elegance of the St. Regis roof garden. I liked it very much but was concerned when the banquet manager quoted the prices for the centerpieces, the flowers for the bar, the luncheon menu, the hors d'oeuvres and many other incidentals and extras. Eleanor assured me that she would orchestrate the event and could bring the cost down to the budget I felt comfortable with—and she did. I think this is the only event or party Eleanor ever worked within a budget. One very clever thing she did was to buy 20 round wicker baskets and paint them white. She took these to the florist and told him to load them with white daisies and to attach eight white helium balloons with nine-foot strings to each handle. When you walked into the ornate roof garden you were enveloped in flowers and balloons and festivities. It was exciting, simple and elegant, and created a wonderful ambiance for our 13-year-old's Bar Mitzvah. Eleanor also had a separate bar set up with a red and white awning and a sign that said, "Tony's Place," serving soft drinks and pizzas for the kids. They loved it.

Richard and Anthony: Tony's Bar Mitzvah, 1970

The guest list was ecumenical, to say the least. Attending were my brother Terry, his wife Adelaide, and their sons Phillip and Peter; my brother Howard, his wife Peggy, and their children Andy and Pam; my sisters Bette and Jeannie and their husbands, and Dina and Neal Gluckin and Jeanne's daughters, Nina, Lisa, and Linda Robinson; my brother-in-law Marvin and his wife and their sons Robert, Steve, and Lee; my dear in-laws Anna and Philip Meyerson, and 25 of Tony and Patty's friends. We were friends at that time with an international group of artists, entrepreneurs, designers, and diplomats. (As I had stated before, we worked hard and played hard.) This eclectic group, along with assorted business friends, aunts, uncles, old dear friends, high fashion models, and mad men in advertising, completed the guest list. We all had a wonderful time. It was truly a day to remember forever.

My 50th Birthday – 1978, June

In 1978, Eleanor gave a surprise 50th birthday party for me in Atlantic City. She planned the entire event, working with Bob Block, my closest friend, on the details. This was the period when Atlantic City was first beginning to open big gaming casinos. There was a master plan whereby Atlantic City was to be transformed from a rundown decrepit city into a vibrant casino city, like a smaller Las Vegas. The party was to be held at the first casino to be completed, Bally International, and we had about 50 people who came for the weekend event. The rooms of the hotel were not yet finished, so we stayed across the street at the Holiday Inn. In fact, the only thing Bally's had up and running was part of the casino, so the banquet was held at the Holiday Inn as well. Bob worked with the banquet manager of the Holiday Inn, who was supposed to do the following: 1) have arrangements of very fresh French garden flowers in enormous wicker baskets placed around the room, 2) have crudités and various shellfish hors d'oeuvres passed by white-gloved waiters, and an oyster and clam bar with men opening the crustaceans as ordered, and 3) a pianist to play during the cocktail hour. What we received was nothing remotely like what Eleanor had ordered and paid for. There were no garden flowers, no wicker baskets, no white-gloved waiters, no crudités, no clam and oyster bar, etc., etc. Instead we got red gladiolas laid out on three-foot-tall stanchions across three eight-foot aluminum tables. They looked as though they'd come from a mob funeral earlier in the day (which they well might have). The waiters looked like hoods (maybe they were) and the crudités were so overcooked they were like mush. The piano player left after 20 minutes to take his "union break" and never returned. Eleanor's elegant affair was anything but. Still, the laughter that continued from Saturday night through Sunday brunch created a sensational and hysterically funny surprise birthday party for me.

Our 30th Wedding Anniversary – 1986, December

Our 30th anniversary party was held on a Sunday night at the Four Seasons restaurant. Those of you who know Eleanor know that of course it was black tie. The restaurant and grill room of the Four Seasons were closed on Sunday evenings, so this was the perfect time. We planned the event with one of the owners, Paul Kovi, who was a delightful man and a pleasure to work with. (We have since become very good friends with his then-partner, Tom Margittai, who lives near us on Tano Road in Santa Fe, although we did not know Tom at that time.)

We decided to take over the entire restaurant, including the grill room, the bar, and the pool room. For hors d'oeuvres, Eleanor created several international tasting tables, each with a special canopy and motif decorated in the style of the country it represented, including Japan, China, Thailand, France, Morroco, Turkey and Italy. The servers were grandly turned out in the costumes of the various countries. The entire bar area looked like a culinary United Nations, and the food was delicious. After hors d'oeuvres, we walked through the great hall, with its fabulous Picasso needlepoint, into the pool room. It is called the "pool room" because in the center of this extraordinary, simple and elegant space was a white marble pool. Eleanor had a clear Lucite floor put over the pool for dancing and surrounded the pool on all sides with masses of white amaryllis, white hyacinth and white freesia. She requested that the orchestra be placed on a balcony overlooking the room. The effect was utterly simple and ultra chic. Our children, their best friends, immediate and extended family members and our friends comprised the guest list. A lot of our friends were involved with Wall Street, fashion, restaurants, real estate, newspapers, politics and the arts. They all came. The party was a huge success. Most importantly, Eleanor and I had a wonderful time.

Patricia Elin Brenner

Patricia's Wedding – 1990, May

Patricia was married on the Fifth of May to Mark Frederick Jackson at an extraordinary place—The Metropolitan Club at 60th Street and Fifth Avenue in New York City. This is an old, very prestigious club founded in 1891 by JP Morgan when he was refused membership to the Knickerbocker Club. The outside of the building is white marble and limestone. It was designed by the most famous architect of his time, Stanford White. The club itself has several floors. On the main floor, overlooking Fifth Avenue, is a very large room called the reading room with huge steel-grey marble fireplaces at each end, gilt moldings, gold frieze and allegorical paintings on the ceilings. Pat was married to Mark in this magnificent room. Since the room itself was extraordinarily ornate, Eleanor decided that she absolutely did not want flowers to "gild the lily." She ordered gold ballroom chairs with pale grey cushions, and 18 custom-built five-foot-tall pale grey Doric wood columns. The columns, which were lined up along the aisle, were decorated with 8-inch-wide cream-colored candles ranging from 10 to 24 inches in height and had heavy gold rope tied around them reaching to the floor. Patricia's gown was gorgeous and I was so very proud to walk my beautiful daughter Patty down the aisle. Patty's bridesmaids wore beautiful, simple, elegant, cream-colored silk crepe and chiffon column dresses. Mark's groomsmen wore white tie and tails. For the "huppah" Eleanor had four enormous ficas trees brought in and tied them two-thirds of the way up with heavy gold rope, leaving an opening at the top for G D to view the couple. She completed this with a table covered in four floor-length cloths of cream-colored silk organza. She stressed that the table holding the glass and the wine had to look like it was floating on a cloud. It did. There were 180 guests, as the ballroom could not hold any more. Among the guests were family, extended family, our dear friends and Patty and Mark's friends. It certainly was a group of beautiful people.

After the ceremony, the wedding party and guests went to the rotunda, with its two marble, circular staircases, for the receiving line, where we were served champagne and hors d'oeuvres. Eleanor had two major floral arrangements created. The first one was at the inside entrance to the rotunda and the second was placed on a baroque table holding the seating cards in the large hall on the third floor leading to the grand dining room. For the dinner dance Eleanor coordinated an arrangement of white orchids, white freesia and white lilies to compliment the masses of white French tulips on the dinner tables. It was definitely over the top.

Anthony and Richard: The Metropolitan Club, Patricia's Wedding, 1990

Patricia Elin Brenner

Walking Down the Aisle

The orchestra we engaged for the dinner dance was outstanding and played until 1:30 in the morning at Patty and Mark's request. "Ka ching...Ka ching." But the cherry on the cake of the "Ka Ching" was Sylvia Weintraub's bill for the wedding cake. Sylvia considered herself the Picasso, the Balanchine and the Mies van der Rohe of the event cake business and her bills were commensurate. She was very proud that at every society wedding in New York she was the chosen one to create "the cake." The price? Don't ask. If you need to ask, you shouldn't buy one.

Mr. and Mrs. Mark Frederick Jackson

Eleanor's Birthday Party – 1996, March

I must tell you about a wonderful party that I gave for Eleanor's birthday in 1996 at the Mark Hotel in New York City. Our sensational nephew Raymond Bickson, who was at that time the head of the Mark Hotel, had organized and orchestrated two other parties for Eleanor's birthdays but this was the *pièce de résistance*. Of course it was black tie and glamorous beyond words. For the cocktail hour Raymond had magnums of champagne continually flowing, a caviar bar ensconced in an ice swan, and a myriad of hors d'oeuvres. Dinner was in a wonderfully decorated room. It was delicious and the wines that accompanied it were superb, but *le dernier cri* was the gold-swathed ceiling and walls of another room which Ray had set up as a Parisian Boite with tiny cocktail tables and chairs all covered in gossamer gold tulle. If this wasn't enough, Raymond had engaged an absolute double of Marilyn Monroe in a skin-tight gold sequined gown to sing "Happy Birthday to You" a la Marilyn and JFK. What a spectacular party! But the topper was that our darling grandson Maxwell Tucker Brenner was born two days later.

My 70ʰ Birthday – 1998, June – a Surprise Party

For my 70th birthday, Eleanor threw a 1928-style gangster party. It was held in a large, private room in the back of El Nido restaurant in Tesuque. We were not yet living full time in Santa Fe, and our residence there was a small charming home which many of our Santa Fe friends said reminded them of a tiny villa in Tuscany. About 100 guests attended the event, all of them characters in a script Eleanor wrote about Chicago circa 1928 with all of the gun molls, dolls and gangsters. Judy and Bob Block, Maxine Pines, my brother Howard, our niece and nephew Connie and Raymond Bickson, Terri and Alfy D'Ancona, and of course our wonderful children, Patty and Mark Jackson and Tony Brenner all flew in for the party. Everyone dressed as their personas in the play and they were fabulous. A few stand out in my mind's eye to this day: Myrna Ruskin, a "doll" hat check girl selling Viagra, Bob Block as Tony Salami, dropping his pants during the evening to gales of laughter, Tom Margittai as a French movie producer, Richard Tang as a knock out gangsta, Connie Bickson, beyond glamorous in her white gown and floor-length white ostrich boa, our handsome Raymond as the suave gangster, Terri D'Ancona as a gorgeous chorus girl, Tony Brenner and Mark Jackson as the gangsters, gangstas, in their white dinner jackets, dark glasses, and machine guns, patting down every guest who entered El Nido. My daughter Patricia was the ultimate knockout flapper along with other great flappers Robin Rubel, Judy Block, Barbara Meyer, Glenna Boyd, and Vicki Stamm. Donald Meyer was the master of ceremonies in his checkered jacket, and John Rubel was outstanding in his gangster regalia, but sadly 10 other gangsters machine-gunned him to death. Oh well…that was Chicago Land 1928.

Da Dolls wid Da Boss

Da Boss' #1 Moll

The Rubels, AKA Johnny da
Joint and Daisy da Doll

Eddie da Executioner wid his favorite moll

Patty and Raymond: the moll and da gansta

Da Dolls and Molls

A Doll wid da Boss

Da gorgeous doll Connie wid da major gansta Ray

Two beautiful dolls: Helene and Connie

NOTABLE VACATIONS

Summers in Westport, Connecticut—1961 – 1964

Westport in those years was a charming small town located on the water in Connecticut. It had a very relaxed and casual lifestyle and was an easy one-hour commute from Manhattan by train or car. We had three wonderful summers there, each time renting a different house. Our children were very young, having been born in 1957 and 1959. Long Shore Country Club had been taken over by the city just prior to our coming and made into a club for residents of Westport. Those who lived in Westport and wished to buy a summer membership at a very reasonable price were able to do just that. The club was a very lovely country club with clay tennis courts, a beach, a large pool, food, etc. and the grounds were very well maintained. Our children had the run of the club, particularly while Eleanor and I played tennis. I played a great deal of tennis those summers, often leaving Bloomingdale's at five to play in the early evenings, and my game was pretty good. Tony and Pat had their cousins Andy and Pam Brenner, Howard and Peggy's children, who were the same ages, and they played together from morning until night. Lots of parties and a very carefree time in our lives and a great bonding time with our children.

St. Tropez with Henri, Summer of 1971

Our week in St. Tropez was just wonderful because our great friend, Henri Martinez, traveled with us. Henri was the very best dancer ever and a French artist who worked in New York. It was because of him that we saw St. Tropez only as someone who knew it so well. Besides his dancing ability, Henri was charming and handsome and no one could say "no" to him. He took us to all the most fun beach clubs, where we would have lunch of fresh-caught fish and wine on the beach under umbrellas or thatched shacks. Each beach club had a certain character that appealed to different lifestyles, ranging from gay to nude to what the French considered a family beach club. We visited them all. It was very interesting. At night we had late dinners at nine, ten, or even eleven, and then went to various bars and discothèques. One morning, towards the end of the week, Henri asked me if he could borrow $500. I said yes and gave him the money. Later that day Henri invited Eleanor and me to a party he was hosting in my honor (with my money). What savoir-faire and what style! Henri took us one night to a gay bar where he decided to put me in a funny and awkward situation. It must have been three o'clock in the morning, when Henri took us to Cinq A Sept, a very small, intimate bar and disco, where his friend Michelle was the maitré d'. Eleanor and Henri were dancing while the very charming and handsome Michelle and I sat on high stools at the bar, talking about life. He suddenly excused himself and disappeared. Several minutes later a beautiful woman with black lace hose, high heels and very long legs came to the bar and plopped herself onto my lap. I was enjoying her until I realized that the beautiful lady was Michelle in drag. That was Henri! He had organized the entire happening. I might add that Eleanor and Henri fell into uncontrollable laughter, as were the other guests at Cinq A Sept. Unfortunately, Henri died from AIDS shortly thereafter. He is truly missed by Eleanor and me.

Eleanor and I played tennis in Beauvallon, since at that time there were no tennis courts in St. Tropez. It was at least an hour's drive by car, but I was not going to miss my tennis. I wanted to play no later than ten in the morning and this was no easy task, as we generally went to bed between three and four. On our first day at Beauvallon, there were two men playing on the next court who began talking with us. They explained that they too were planning to return to St. Tropez and invited us to join them for lunch. One of the men was older and worked for IBM in Paris and the other was a very handsome doctor from Madagascar. We followed them to the beach, which we were surprised to find was a topless family beach. The older man introduced us to his wife. Her breasts showed substantial signs of the effect of gravity. When we sat down to lunch, the younger man's wife joined us. She wore a straw headdress over her long blonde hair, multiple layers of colored beads around her neck and a very skimpy g-string. She was a number 11 (10 being perfect), and was very, very, very sexy. She wanted to sit next to me at lunch. To say the least, I was very distracted.

European Trip Spring/Summer 1975

In honor of his graduation from the Riverdale School in June 1975, Tony requested that the family take a trip together to Europe. Eleanor and I suggested that he might have more fun on a teen group tour, but he was adamant. We planned a month-long trip, organizing the first two and a half weeks around Eleanor's work schedule in London and Paris. I would meet up with the family in Italy for the last ten days as I was very busy running Brenner Couture.

The first stop was Scotland, where there was the slight problem of daylight until two a.m. and sunrise at four a.m. The three of them visited the castles and sites around Edinburgh, and very much enjoyed their stay at the Balmoral Hotel, which was completed in the Victorian style in 1902. Patty thought haggis, the most famous of Scottish cuisine (composed of sheep's offal, lungs, heart and liver mixed with suet and lightly cooked oatmeal, placed inside a sheep's stomach, sewn closed and then boiled) was the most revolting combination of food that she had ever heard of. It rained the four days they were there, but that did not stop the sites, the photographs or the night festivals of the Bagpipers. Patty only wanted to know what the men wore under their kilts. (We now know that they wear nothing!) They went on a shopping trip one afternoon and Tony found a brown suede hunting jacket that he fell in love with. They went to a charming country inn for dinner that evening and Tony was quite proud of his new sartorial splendor. Unfortunately, the waiter spilled the entire tureen of cocky leeky soup all over Tony's new jacket. Since they were leaving Scotland the next morning, there was no opportunity to purchase another one. Believe it or not, Tony on occasion, still mentions that jacket.

They then went on to London, where Eleanor had to work and the kids toured and roamed the city. Tony and Patty very much enjoyed the theatres and dinners, as well as late afternoon tea with Eleanor in the "Palm Court" of the famed Ritz Hotel.

They were off to Paris next, where Eleanor decided they should stay on the Left Bank to give Tony and Patty the flavor of the Paris she loved. When they arrived at the Hotel Danube on the Rue de Bac, they were greeted by the day manager with three tiny worn out towels and wash cloths, accompanied by a tiny bar of soap. He informed them that they were to use these during their four day stay. As Patty said, that was the best thing about the hotel. Patty asked Eleanor, "How did we end up in this dump?" The shower head fell off with every shower, the door knob to the bathroom did not work so you easily became locked inside and their suite consisted of two beds in one room with a broken bed in an alcove. Eleanor told Patty that in the hotel's brochure the Rockefellers had raved about its charm. Patty asked, "Which Rockefellers?" Eleanor admitted she did not know, and Patty said, "It must have been Sam and Sadie Rockefeller."

Eleanor took the first day in Paris off from work and walked the kids seven miles. They were exhausted, but Eleanor said, "I want you to see Paris at night and the only way to do that is to walk." I do not know the kids' reaction to her comment, but I do know they were mighty happy to see me.

They toured the French countryside, spent three days in the Loire Valley and the Chateau D'Artigny in Montbazon. It is a spectacular Chateau. Unfortunately, during their visit to Chartres, Tony broke his nose by walking into a plate-glass door as they were leaving a boulangerie, which Eleanor proceeded to set with ice in a bar. (I broke my nose the same way—like father, like son.) When I finally met up with my family in Capri, Tony's nose looked fine, but unfortunately he could not breathe.

They continued to tour France by car from Chateau D'Artigny to Provence, where they stayed at Beaumaniere, another incredible chateau. They then proceeded to Carcassonne, a medieval walled city, but they felt it was touristy. Patty described the famed cassoulet as "not fit for human consumption" and said they might want to "feed it to their pigs!"

Capri – Lake Como

Capri was a wonderful place for me to join the family. It was charming and beautiful, yet very casual and relaxed. The Quisisana Hotel was small, intimate and charming. As you entered the hotel, there was an outdoor seating area on the main drag for drinks and snacks where you could watch the world going by while imbibing. There were no cars allowed on the island of Capri since it was so small, but everything was close and you could easily walk to your destinations. The first thing Tony and I did was to scout out the local tennis courts. We found six clay courts side by side in a stadium type of building, where there were young ball boys who picked up your balls after each point, so that you did not have to do anything but play. It was quite hot for tennis, so the ball boys really served a good purpose. At night, dining quite late, we went to the various charming small restaurants, all outdoors, most of them off the main drag. We had delicious, excellent meals. Following dinner, we would walk along the main shopping street, where the ladies completed their continual shopping in the famed boutiques of Capri.

We then travelled to Villa D'este. Villa D'este is one of my most favorite places in Europe. It is picturesque and the hotel is exquisite. The grounds of the hotel have incredibly beautiful terraces, with beautiful and glorious gardens. For me, though, the best part was the magnificent tennis courts. It was probably the finest tennis facility I have ever played at. On the terraced courts, you were not only surrounded by grass and beautiful gardens, but also had views of Lake Como. There were four courts in all, two courts located side by side on each of two elevated terraces. It was very difficult to totally concentrate on tennis with all that beauty.

Eleanor's Birthday in Venice, Italy – 1976

Eleanor's birthday in March of 1976 was celebrated with a surprise weekend in Venice. It was cold and rainy when we arrived in Venice and it remained that way throughout our stay. The Airlines lost our luggage, so we had no clothes other than those we wore traveling. Eleanor's make-up was also in the lost luggage. I told her, "With your skin, you don't need make-up!" We stayed at the Hotel Danielli, which was elegant and beautiful. How would we dress? The first thing we did was buy four gorgeous white Italian dress shirts in my size. (Eleanor and I each wore one of the shirts during the day, then we sent those to the hotel laundry and wore the other two clean shirts for the evening.) Then we went to a hat store and bought two "Borsalino" Fedoras, which were very chic at the time and necessary because of the continuous rain. Now we were in business. We walked all over Venice and took many, many gondola rides because Eleanor loved the gondoliers' romantic songs. Particularly astounding was Piazza San Marco (in English, St. Mark's Square). It is huge, and on a normal holiday would be filled with thousands of people but since it was grey and raining heavily it was totally empty of people except for us. We walked all around the square in the pouring rain and ended in a tiny café for very, very hot chocolate. I do not need to tell anyone, since you all know, that the Italian food was excellent. To further celebrate Eleanor's birthday, I surprised her with a magnificent star sapphire ring. The stone was huge, 67 karat, and it was surrounded by diamonds. She was totally shocked and thrilled. For those of you who know Eleanor, you understand that she likes big. It was the most romantic weekend. (At 5 am on Tuesday, as we were leaving, our luggage appeared.) We left Venice in the pouring rain to go to Milano and Bergamo where Eleanor designed cotton knit dresses for our sportswear business.

During the summer of 1983, Eleanor was very busy with her business in Hong Kong so I decided I would meet up with Tony, who had completed Stanford Business School and was travelling around Europe before he started his new job. I was to meet him on a certain day at the Hotel Du Cap in Cap Ferat. Unfortunately, I had to postpone the trip by two days due to what I thought was a business crisis. In actuality, the problem was still there when I returned to Wall Street two weeks later. I learned that one should never postpone pleasure to deal with business problems because invariably the problem is resolved by others or waits for your return. We did not have cell phones, so all I could do was to leave Tony messages at the hotel, letting him know that I would be delayed.

When I finally met up with Tony (two days late) he was very agitated. He had a met a beautiful Norwegian girl, Gunvor, in Greece and had fallen in love. Because of my delay, he'd had to kiss her goodbye two days earlier than need be. He said he could have brought her along and had a great extra couple of days with her. Tony and Gunvor spoke regularly for nearly a year, but the logistics were too difficult to overcome. Now back to our trip. Things began looking up for Tony when he discovered I had rented a BMW stick shift car. He was in seventh heaven driving such a high-performance vehicle. One day, driving back from St. Tropez, I fell sound asleep as he began to drive. When I awoke I was astounded that we had made the trip in such a short time. Thereafter on our trip I called him AJ Foyt, a renowned racecar driver at the time.

We stayed that night at Hotel Du Cap, which was too stodgy and old for Tony, and for me too. One interesting event occurred while we were at the hotel. Just before we were to leave, we saw the King of Jordan walking around the outside of the hotel, surrounded by 15-20 bodyguards. We left early the next morning for St. Tropez. The first thing we did every day in St. Tropez was enjoy *chausson au pomme*, marvelous espressos and cappuccinos, and then head for the tennis courts in Beauvallon.

After tennis we would go to the beach and admire the scenery, being sure to visit all the beaches from nude to "conservative." We would then eat fresh fish on the beach in the shade of an awning or simple wood structure. The fish was always delectable and of course, in France, we always had wine with lunch. We would then sober up and relax until dinner time, which in St. Tropez was very late. Following this we'd go to a discothèque where we danced until early morning and then came home and collapsed.

We had a super time together and really bonded. I recommend that every father try to take a vacation alone with his son. Not as a father/son but just as two guys having a good time together. I told Eleanor that Tony and I never looked for trouble, nor did we ever get into trouble. She just laughed.

Ibiza, Spain – Summer 1989

Ibiza is a small resort island off the coast of Spain, just a short flight from Barcelona. I flew in from New York and Eleanor from Hong Kong. Ibiza has a very gay atmosphere, in more ways than one. There was quite a group of us that flew from the U.S., including Patty, her then boyfriend Mark Jackson, Tony, and three designer friends of Eleanor: Thad, Kathy and Karen. Thad was gay and adventuresome, a pied piper. He was always on the go and was a fabulous master of ceremonies, always planning dinners, drinks, shows, etc. During the day, we basically stayed at our hotel, an extraordinarily charming Mediterranean inn located in the hills above the city. We sunned around the pool and swam constantly. At the hotel I saw one of the most beautiful girls ever. She was a German secretary, and her companion was a German industrialist. She had the most gorgeous green eyes and always swam in the nude. Not bad scenery! At nine o'clock in the evenings we would go into town by car for shopping and cocktails. Our timing director and pied piper, Thad, would make all the arrangements for dinner and dancing. Dinner was late, around 11 p.m. or midnight, since Ibiza in the summer was an all-night proposition. After dinner, at about one or two a.m., we would all go to the local discothèque, which was outside and adjacent to the beach and ocean. The disco was huge and easily held more than 1,000 people, who would be dancing to the hottest rhythm of continuous music. Eleanor was concerned how our conservative son-in-law to-be, Mark, would react to the wild people from New York's fashion crowd and to the crazy people in town, but they all got along just great and everything was perfect!

Our friend Barbara had a spectacular home in Ibiza, part of which had been built in the fifteenth century. She gave a fabulous party for us with champagne and caviar and every other outrageous delicacy you could imagine. In addition she and her husband, Lucien, arranged a wonderful day of sailing for all of us. We were to sail out of the harbor and go to a small island where they had ordered a very large paella for the group. It was a beautiful day with great fun and the best paella fresh from the sea. It was a spectacular moment to remember.

The week in Ibiza was truly wonderful! Shortly after our trip Thad died from AIDS. We mourned our charming, delightful and courageous friend. Eleanor and I still talk about him to this day.

Mauna Kea, February, 1982 – 1989

During the 1980s, Eleanor's business required her to live and work six months a year in Hong Kong. The collections of EPB Easy, TPR and the main designer label, Eleanor P Brenner, were sold in very large specialty department stores such as Saks Fifth Avenue, Bloomingdale's, Neiman Marcus and Nordstrom's, and Eleanor P. Brenner had its own departments in Neiman Marcus. The magazine Town & Country named Eleanor one of the top ten fashion designers in America for 12 straight years. A great customer of Eleanor's was a store on Oak Street in Chicago named Terri D. It was owned and managed by a beautiful and charming woman, Terri D'Ancona. Every January and early February, Eleanor was in Hong Kong designing her fall collection. She worked exceptionally hard to have everything (samples, designs, fabrics) in place so the correct flow would work. In addition, she checked styles that were in production for spring delivery. Every year at the end of January or beginning of February, Chinese New Year takes place. All the factories and commercial businesses stop working in Hong Kong and everything closes down for two weeks. We would plan a holiday at Mauna Kea, on the Big Island of Hawaii, during that time. We would meet Terri and Alfy D'Ancona, now our dear friends, and spend a week with them at the Mauna Kea Hotel. To reach the hotel, you flew into Honolulu and then transferred to a smaller plane bound for the Big Island. The Mauna Kea Hotel is on the west side of the island, sheltered by the mountains that separate the west from the east and block off most of the rain, so that we were assured of fine weather. We played lots of tennis, Alfy and Eleanor against Terri and me, and had great competition and fun. Alfy and I also played singles. There was a beautiful golf course located along the ocean and we walked there in the early morning with Terri and Alfy, before enjoying an enormous breakfast in our rooms or at the hotel's very special buffet. Eleanor and I walked along the gorgeous beach during the day as well, and I swam in the ocean or at the pool.

There were four restaurants in the hotel and most nights we ate at one with a beautiful terrace overlooking the Pacific Ocean. Before dinner, we would go to the bar adjacent to the terrace, where Alfy and I would dive into the best fried shrimp I'd ever had and proceed to demolish them. Our trips to Hawaii were fabulous, fun and very romantic.

Within a year or so a large group of the D'Anconas' friends from Chicago started joining us in Hawaii. We became a large group of 10 to 12 people. John Hart was one of the group and he is still a good friend of ours living part-time in Santa Fe. He was in the wine auction business and would bring wine that we would drink at sunset on the beach. I would bring caviar from Macy's, the famous department store in New York City on 34th Street. We would all carouse on the beach until the sun finally set and then return to our rooms to bathe and dress before regrouping for more libations and dinner. The visits to Mauna Kea were welcome respites from our pressure-filled, peripatetic lifestyles, and we always returned to New York City or Hong Kong after those vacations with renewed energy.

After eleven years, Richard-san decided to visit his geisha in Hong Kong. Rudi Greiner, the GM of the Regent Hotel, was so overwhelmed that he gave the shogun / Richard-san and his geisha Eleanor the grand suite at the Regent Hong Kong to honor Richard-san's long-awaited arrival.

Egypt & Israel Trip, Summer 1980

Eleanor and I had discussed our Egypt and Israel trip for three months preceding our travels. We wanted Patty and Tony not only to see but to truly understand Israel, the Jewish homeland. We flew to Geneva, Switzerland, where we had six hours to spare before we left for Egypt. Eleanor had planned a site-seeing trip around Geneva, but Tony had a terrible stomach ache so instead of touring we sat on a bench most of the time, off the street, with him vomiting. This was not an auspicious beginning. It turns out, he was suffering from an early bout of appendicitis which eventually led to an emergency appendectomy in the fall of 1981. This occurred just before his first semester exams at Stanford Business School and made for a lot of excitement.

Finally, we were on the plane to Cairo, Egypt. Upon our arrival we engaged a taxi to drive us to the Menna House Hotel. It was quite a ride with traffic the likes of which I had never witnessed before. New York City traffic jams were nothing compared to Cairo's crawl; it seemed that we proceeded only inches at a time. We finally arrived at the Menna House, which was a big sprawling hotel with large grounds and tennis courts. It was famous for its extraordinary views of the pyramids, which could be seen from our hotel rooms and were especially magical at dawn and dusk. We had a car and driver take us everywhere because of both the extreme overcrowding and the poverty of the people who would surround us for baksheesh whenever we left the hotel. The poverty and filth were everywhere, and the destitute and hungry condition of the people colored all that you saw. We visited the Cairo museum, which was horribly hot, even with all the windows wide open, and filthy dirty.

After three days in Cairo, we travelled up the Nile River by boat for six days. It was very interesting to see how the Nile was the focal point of the people's lives—everything from drinking water, washing clothes, bathing, defecating (you get the idea). Most of the people on the shore were beggars. The long robes worn by the men were disgustingly dirty. The food on the boat was only adequate, but at least we did not get sick. Eleanor, Tony and Patricia took a side trip that I passed on to Abu Simbel, which turned out to be one of the highlights of their Egyptian Trip. They flew to Abu Simbel on a day when the heat was so intense that the ice water they had started with became hot enough to brew tea before they returned. They were overwhelmed with the beauty and enormity of the two sculptures of the Pharaoh Ramses II and his wife Nefertiti, which he had built in the 13th century BC. We returned to Cairo for a day, then on to Israel.

The Israeli trip was a first for all of us. We were overwhelmingly impressed. Israel cannot be truly understood and appreciated until you visit it in person. One has to travel around this country that has been carved out of the desert by the sheer determination and guts of the Israelis. The country is very small with two major cities—Jerusalem and Tel Aviv—surrounded by kibbutzes and small towns. In fact, it is so small that you can drive from one end of the country to the other end in several hours and in some ways this flexibility has helped the Israelis defend their country. We arrived in Tel Aviv and we were driven to the King David Hotel in Jerusalem. The hotel is deeply steeped in the history and lore of Israel. We hired an Israeli driver and guide, who was recommended to us by our dear friend Rena Blumberg, for our week in Israel. He was exceptionally verbal and knowledgeable about the country's history, politics and mores. He never stopped talking, but we learned a great deal from him.

The King David Hotel was very charming and very open. It was a central location from which we could see and visit many of the historic sites. We walked a great deal in Jerusalem to get the amazing feeling of how ancient the city is. We visited the Jewish museum, the Mount of Olive, the Western Wall, Yad Vashem, temples, Knesset, and on and on.

I had hoped to develop clients in Israel for D.H. Blair. Prior to the trip I contacted the minister in charge of economic development. He arranged for many companies to visit with me in his office while I was in Israel. He also had several companies visit with me when they came to the U.S. after I returned to New York City. No deals developed from these introductions, primarily because the Israeli entrepreneurs had an exaggerated sense of the value of their businesses and were relatively inflexible and unwilling to adjust their valuations. This, in my opinion, priced most of them out of the U.S. marketplace. I also talked to them about the Weitzman Institute and Ben Gurion University and future possibilities, since Israel had very advanced breakthrough technologies, but nothing ever came of it. Maybe I was a year or two or ten too early, since they have since developed into one of the most important sources of technology in the world.

Of course, one of the first places we visited was Yad Vashem, which is the museum and memorial of the Holocaust. The museum does a wonderful job in presenting what occurred and it is heart-wrenching. We visited several kibbutzes and swam in the Dead Sea, which was unlike any water I had ever been in. It had a strange odor and was very debilitating. Literally, all you could do was float. When we left from Tel Aviv to return to New York City, we were astounded by the time and thoroughness that was required before you could board the plane, including being examined and taken to a private room for more thorough screening. No wonder Israel has prevented terrorist acts on their air flights.

We all left Israel with much greater pride, respect and admiration for what this wonderful, small country has accomplished. After the ravages of the Jewish Holocaust, in 1948 Israel became the homeland for the Jewish nation. With over six million Jews killed during World War II and the survivors with no place to go and no country to take them in, the Jewish people carved out of the desert a thriving, independent country that offered citizenship to all Jews seeking a homeland. Israel also became the beacon and center for Jews all over the world. (I believe that "As Israel goes, so go the Jews worldwide.")

SANTA FE, NEW MEXICO

Although Eleanor and I did not permanently move to Santa Fe until 2000, the wheels were set in motion back in the 70s, when I expressed my desire to see the western part of the United States. (Previously most of our vacations had been spent in Europe or on the East Coast). Eleanor agreed, and for two summers we visited Santa Fe, Sun Valley, the Grand Tetons, Jackson Hole, Yellowstone National Park, Yosemite National Park and other well-known American landmarks. (As an aside, at Yellowstone National Park, we parked our car in the massive parking facility. Many hours later, we returned to the area but had totally forgotten the color of our rental car. Needless to say, we spent endless hours searching.) One of the unique things that I learned from the trip, from the young people we had met from Boise, Idaho, was that people from the west took great pride and pleasure in our land, the sky, the mountains and water. We particularly loved the Grand Tetons in Jackson Hole, Wyoming. We went fishing in Jackson Lake and caught fish for our dinner that night. Nothing tastes like the fresh fish you caught that day.

We were overwhelmed by the Redwoods and the Sequoia trees, the tallest trees in the world, that we saw while driving through Yosemite National Park in California. Our country is truly a blessed country with all of its magnificence and majesty.

Eleanor fell in love with the Sangre de Cristo mountains and their constantly changing colors. At that time, Santa Fe was a sleepy New Mexico town with dirt roads and virtually no traffic. In town there was not one traffic light, but in the plaza there were four hitching posts for your horses. We stayed at Bishop's Lodge, which was very nice but not really special. I thought it was like an old age home. Little did I realize, at that time, that some day we would be very happy living in Santa Fe.

Fast forward about thirteen years: Our good friends, Myrna and Ron Ruskin, were thinking of buying a house in Santa Fe, New Mexico. I never knew at that time that Eleanor had made a mental note, from our previous and only trip to Santa Fe, that some day she would like to live in Santa Fe, or as she said, "I have had an epiphany that I will spend the end of my life in Santa Fe." We both were very busy in 1986. I was on Wall Street and Eleanor's business was booming. Eleanor was in touch with a prominent local broker in Santa Fe, and through the broker bought a small house in the hills off Bishop's Lodge Road, above Fort Marcy Park. As a matter of fact, she bought the house while in Thailand, sight unseen, and when I met her in Hawaii, she told me she had made a bid but did not know if the bid had been accepted. I said, "How could you have made such an irresponsible purchase?" We agreed that if we did not like the house we would turn around and sell it. Although I was upset by the way it was purchased, I liked the house more than Eleanor did. Subsequently she converted the house, which had been a model for the developer, into a small Tuscan villa. This was the start of our Santa Fe adventure and maybe the fulfillment of our destiny.

We spent the first year not having time to go to Santa Fe. The second year, two weeks. The third year, a little more time. In fact, the house was so little used that Eleanor kept giving it away, even to people that she did not know very well. In the 90s our children both settled in California permanently, and Eleanor suggested moving to Santa Fe as our new home.

The decision to look around for a new property took us to many locations in Santa Fe, but none had the spectacular view that we were looking for. Finally we saw the property that we were to end up buying. It was located on a dirt road, on a ridge off of Tano Road. To me this was a major problem since I objected strenuously to a house located on a dirt road since it becomes very muddy whenever it rains or snows thus causing slipping and sliding. In addition, your car is constantly covered in dust and dirt, all permeating into your garage and home. Eleanor found the property in the summer of 1995 and we looked at it several times, but I passed on it because of the dirt road. The view was spectacular. We had 180-degree vistas with literally no houses between us and the mountains. Eleanor loved the land and we had a choice from the seller of any of the four lots the property had been zoned for. We decided on plat number one, which was 12.8, acres and 7300 feet above sea level, without any other houses blocking the view of the Sangre de Cristo mountains to the East, the Jemez mountains to the West, and the badlands to the North. The land was so important to Eleanor and was so beautiful that I swallowed my reluctance and said let's go ahead. (Fast forward to 2005. I was finally able to convince the county to put in a one and a half mile paved road and I went to the state legislature to get it approved. An asphalt road was constructed and we, and all our neighbors, are thrilled that we have it, including Arlena and Martin Markinson who walk their dog every day on a much better surface. This road not only had the obvious advantages but in addition was much safer and increased the value of our property.)

Eleanor showing Dick where his new home is going to be

DESIGN AND CONSTRUCTION
OF THE HOUSE, 1996–2000

Eleanor started constructing our dream house while I was recovering from Dr. Ranawat's surgical revision of my right hip. Dr. Wilson had blown the first surgery by using a biodegradable concept which was to have the implant adhere to the bone via the bio material. The prosthesis came loose in four years and was very painful. Revisions are complex and difficult procedures and a lot of orthopedists will not perform them except on their own previous work. Since you must remove the old prosthesis and split additional bone before you can replace the existing replacement, most surgeons are very negative about this operation. And there was Eleanor, while I was recovering from surgery in the hospital and at home, designing at all hours of the day and night, making all kinds of drawings and detailing elevations, composition and surfaces. Eleanor knew exactly what she wanted, a warm, great home for us and for our entire family to enjoy and desire to visit very often, and for great parties. That's just what we achieved. Her designs were then given to Peter Wurzburger, who did the architectural work and the blue prints with all the specifications and detailing. Peter came up with a splendid suggestion, that we not build a separate guest house because of the topography of the building plot, but instead place the guest house under the main house. This was a brilliant suggestion and overcame a serious road block to moving forward. Peter was wonderful to work with—a really good guy. He and his wife Maureen Brooks became close friends. Unfortunately, we had a construction manager who was a disaster. We terminated her forty percent into the job but not before she made some horrific mistakes. Probably the most serious one was the plumber she hired from Albuquerque, who, I think, was not a plumber but really a shoemaker. To this day, most of the problems in the ten years we have lived here have been plumbing and heating related. The other serious problem was the septic system. We had to replace the entire septic system two years after it had been installed. Santa Fe County is tough to build in and there are endless delays brought about by regulation and the multiple refilings that are necessary to gain approval.

Eleanor also, in our design, had developed two apartments for some of our staff to live in, which has worked out very well. In addition, she designed a separate storage building on the opposite side of the courtyard from our house and behind that a greenhouse. Eleanor now thinks she made a mistake that the storage area is too small. She gives parties for hundreds—and I mean, literally, hundreds—of guests so she needs a warehouse, and even that might not be big enough. However, we ended up with one of the most beautiful houses in Santa Fe, and no one builds without some problems. We believe that we are truly blessed to live in such beautiful surroundings, and hardly a day goes by that we do not make comments about how blessed and how very grateful we are. Mabel Leyba has a green thumb, and everything she planted (trees, bushes, flowers) at the time of building has grown big and added much beauty to our home. I believed that once we had finished the house, that would be it, but instead it is a work in progress. I ask, when will we be finished, and Eleanor's answer is "soon." We started the house in 1996 and completed it four years later in 2000.

1997, 1998, 1999, 2000 Hacienda de la Vida under construction.
Eleanor bundled up during all those winters.

About five years ago, in 2005, Eleanor started campaigning for a sun room. She calls it that. I call it a small house because it has a kitchen, a full bath and an enormous room with a large entry hall and circular staircase connecting it to our guest house and also to our bedroom. Eleanor also had an elevator installed. Anyway, it turned out great, and I'm very happy with the results. We often use it for poker games with Russ, Lee, Richard R., Don M., Don C., Eddie G., Jerry C., Donn D., and Marty M., for TV viewing, for entertaining and cocktails before dinner, and as a sun room on cold winter days, when it is especially wonderful. Eleanor told me she thought I would enjoy a small south-facing terrace on the winter days. I said okay. Have you ever heard of a 900-square-foot terrace and a 1,500 square-foot-addition, called a sun room and small terrace? Don't ask!!

The house was especially designed with a very large courtyard for the purpose of giving big parties. We did and do exactly that. Pearl Mesta was in all her glory as the hostess with the mostess in Washington D.C. and then came Gwendolyn Cafritz, but she has been displaced by Eleanor P Brenner, who became the new central party giver in Santa Fe. Her motto is "the bigger the better." You have the picture, I'm sure. Be a very close friend, have a birthday, and you will be offered a party. Two of our grandchildren, Alex and Max, love parties, and when they are visiting, there are always several parties scheduled. They pitch right in to help circulate and be charming and talkative and cannot wait to come for these events. (In fact this Christmas/New Year's week we have a party scheduled for over two hundred and fifty guests.) In spring and summer we give enormous parties outdoors in the courtyard. Many of our parties are black tie evenings for which Eleanor has raised the bar of dress and jewels so that the women can happily dress to kill and men can bitch. But, she has succeeded and everyone wishes to come to a Brenner black-tie evening party or a costume ball.

To most people a dinner party is six to ten people. A large dinner party may be 10 to 16 and a major party is 40 to at most 100 guests. Somehow, somewhere, these numbers never reached Eleanor.

When we were building the house, I never realized why the gallery was so big. I envisioned our grandsons, who were very young at the time, riding their bikes there in bad weather. Eleanor had another concept.

My first inkling of Eleanor's concept for Santa Fe parties took place five weeks after 589 packing crates and furniture arrived at Hacienda de la Vida. (The last thing I remember about our beautiful apartment at 1185 Park Avenue was the chaos of floor to ceiling crates and total dismemberment of our wonderful home of forty years.)

Eleanor tells everyone that the reason our marriage of 54 years has survived is because I hate change. Well, I must admit that there is some truth to that statement. As only Eleanor can do, she went into superwoman power mode, because she was determined that our first party, which was being given in honor of our very dear friends Robin and John Rubel, would be beautiful, great fun and delightful. The fact that there were still 25 to 40 workers completing stone work, fireplaces, floors and fountains, not to mention electricity and plumbing and unpacking, was not going to be a deterrent according to Eleanor. As I walked into the kitchen early one morning, I was horror struck. Ye gads! There was a new mountain of crates from Mexico containing what looked to be a thousand dishes. Well, my calculation was pretty close and I said, rhetorically, "What are these dishes for?"

"Darling," said Eleanor, "aren't these fabulous? I designed them, and Mabel and I went to Mexico to have them made."

"But, what for?" I asked.

"Well, John and Robin's party has over 100 guests attending and I thought it would be wonderful to have divine Talavera on the tables for all four courses."

"Talavera? What the hell is Talavera?" I asked.

The party was indeed wonderful. Eleanor had engaged a 15-piece Mariachi band and although the stone floor in the courtyard was not finished, actually not yet started, the rest of the courtyard was a magical combination of flowers, plants and 100 candle-lit lanterns. We even have a notebook with the text and illustrations from the "roast" I gave.

Eleanor worked with her "people" until three a.m. after the party, at which time she had to pack because we were on a seven a.m. flight to New York for her third phase of dental surgery. And thus began the beginning of untold, innumerable parties at Hacienda de La Vida (The House of Life). (As an aside, bless Robin and John for helping to organize and place the cases of books going into our library. They have always been there for us.)

I must admit that each dinner party, whether tiny, with as few as eight guests, or major, with 200 to 350 guests, is always beautiful, the food always wonderful, and the decorations, including newly designed dishes, glassware and accessories for each major party, always spectacular. Eleanor does all the cooking for our dinner parties, except for those with over 150 people.

Since I do not want to overload our reader, I will only tell you about two of Eleanor's major parties, which were given for me, one for my 75th birthday and the other for my 80th birthday.

Patricia and Eleanor, the night before the Africa party

THE AFRICAN PARTY

The theme of my 75th birthday party was Africa. One of Eleanor's great charms is not only living in the moment, but also recreating herself to be an integral part of that moment. When we traveled to Africa, Eleanor's daily outfits consisted of riding pants, boots, shirts, suede safari jackets, flowing silk scarves and a "planters hat," all reminiscent of Africa in the 20s and 30s. In the evening, Eleanor would arrive on our varying terraces in long flowing caftans. During our four and a half weeks in Africa on four different safaris, Eleanor would regale me with stories about Happy Valley, the intrigues of Nairobi, the royal Brits, the other royals from Europe and the super rich daughters of American business titans. "Darling," said Eleanor upon our return from Africa, "You were born in 1928, and I know just exactly the party I am giving for your 75th."

To regress for a moment, the 1920s gangster party for my 70th birthday had 100 guests and was super fun. Eleanor had written a script with loads of characters from Chicago in the 20s. Now she was going to write, plan, design and orchestrate my 75th You guessed it! Nairobi, Kenya 1928. Africa Africa Africa!

Eleanor wrote and rewrote a script for 220 characters. As with everything else in her life, she became totally involved with her created characters, their habits, their foibles, their weaknesses, their glamour, their substance abuse, their brutal instincts, their louche ways and their lifestyles. She designed pre-invitations to find out who was definitely coming, because each guest was to be a persona of her creation and choosing. During this time (about two years), Eleanor was designing African dishes, tortoiseshell stemware and black and silver onyx-inspired flatware. Cases and cases of handmade baskets along with 50 handmade mud cloths arrived from Africa.

Please know, dear reader, that this did not interfere with the twenty or so other parties that we gave during those two years, because Eleanor would say, "It's only thirty-eight guests." As an aside, I must tell you that we have three huge standing freezers in the garages, two very large refrigerators in addition to the four refrigerators and freezers we have in various kitchens, not to mention the refrigerator freezers in the two apartments on the property. During the winter, Eleanor with "one or two or three of her people" cook and bake and carefully label and package everything and store it in the freezers. Over all the years, the only three parties she did not cook for were the first party, my 75th and 80th birthdays.

Eleanor the Duchess of Brenner

Princess Valentina of Denmark with Prince Aigon of Bulgaria
and Richard, the Duke of Brenner

Princess Sophia of Savoy and
Sir Serge Monroe

Mr. Denys Finch Hatton

Lady Alexandra of Chectwick
with Prince Costa of Greece

Lady Lucia Pepperell, Sir Winston Churchill, and Eleanor, the Duchess of Brenner

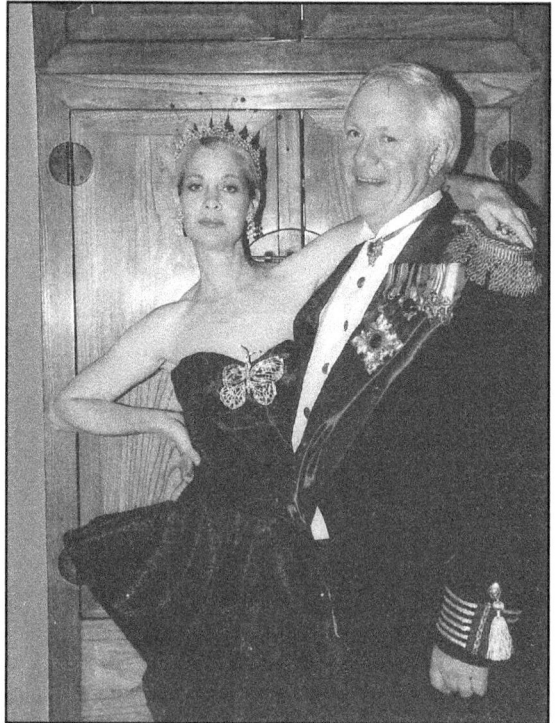

Lady Brett Thutford
with Edward, the
Prince of Wales

The Duke and Duchess of Brenner

The courtyard for the African party was transformed into Nairobi, Kenya 1928. There must have been hundreds of torches lining our long driveway and courtyard. Eleanor said we had to be surrounded by African flowers and African baskets and we were. The tables with their heavy linen drop cloths, mud cloths, tribal inspired napkins, tortoise-shell stemware and African leopard and patterned dishes were superb. Of the 220 guests who accepted the invitation from the Duke of Windsor, 22 had to cancel during the last week due to illness, family crises, etc. But 198 strong boarded the buses in town in front of the main Post Office in full costumery to the astounded looks of tourists and local Santa Feans. I must admit that this African party was spectacular, gorgeous and enormous fun. Eleanor specifically informed all the guests via written correspondence, personal contact and phone messages: "The Duke of Brenner is looking forward to this fantasy evening and begs you to respect his wishes. No gifts please, no speeches and no toasts. Thank you."

ELEANOR'S 70TH BIRTHDAY PARTY

Have you ever met a birthday girl who hand-wrote all the invitations, did all the cooking (with her people), decorated everything in sensational black and white, looked gorgeous, and was her ebullient self? That's my Eleanor.

Happy 70th Birthday, my darling Eleanor

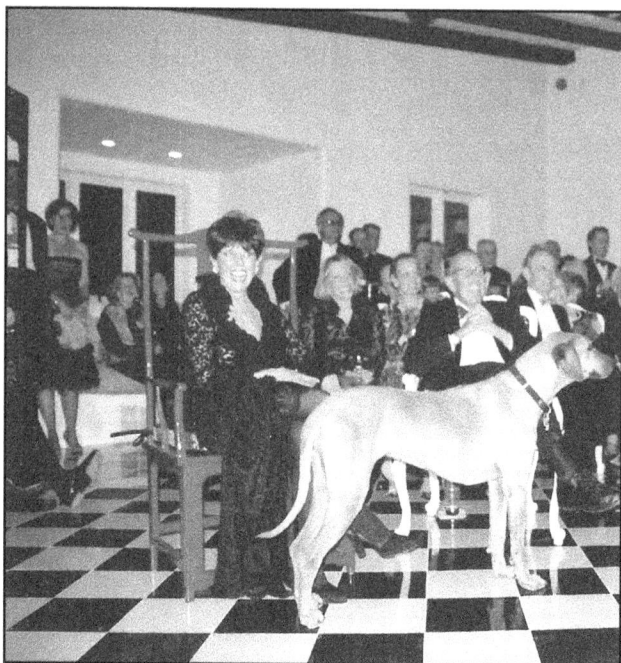

Watching Patricia's video

Dinner for seventy on Eleanor's seventieth

THE INDIA PARTY

Two and half years before my 80th birthday, I started to see books and books arriving in the mail. This is not unusual, as reading is a great pleasure for both of us. However, these books were all about the famous Palaces of India, Maharajahs, Maharanis, Rolls Royces, the yachts of the twenties, the treasures of princes' and the famous tiger and elephant safaris that took place in India in the 20s.

"What's going on?" I asked.

"Darling," said Eleanor. "You know that I have always had a passion to spend time in India. This just does not seem to be in the cards for us, soooo I am bringing India to Santa Fe!"

"How much will it cost?" I asked.

"Oh, it won't be that bad," she said. This is a typical discussion we have about money. No beginning, no middle, and no end. Oil was king at this time and I was heavily invested. This spigot was really flowing and I did not give Eleanor a budget. Of course, I had a wild figure in my mind, but Eleanor most definitely exceeded an unlimited budget.

Arriving from the East coast were special friends and family: Sheila and Arnold Aronson, Judy and Bob Block, Gloria and Phil Cowen, Karen and Jay Eliezar Myrna and Ron Ruskin, my brother Howard and his wife Barbara, my niece and nephew Kathy and Andy Brenner, my niece Dina and her husband Jeff Tranen and my dear brother in law and sister in law Carol and Marvin Meyerson. Also nieces and nephews from the Groveman Clan: Linda, David, Peter, Leslie and Jennifer. Washington DC was represented by Cathy Halverson Testa. From the Midwest: Alfy and Terri D'Ancona from Chicago and Ronnie and Alan Schwartz from Highland Park, Illinois. From the Southwest: Susan and Ron Blankenship, Sherry and John Ferguson, Barbie and Frank Harvey, Audrey and Fred Horne, Marci and Denny McLarry, and Sally and Barney Young. From Mexico: Sarah and José Luis Cateriano. And from Bombay, India, our nieces, the Bickson ladies: Connie, Annick and Alix and our dear friend Birgit Zorniger.

Well, you probably know, the party was beyond spectacular. The 320 guests were astounded by the transformation of our driveway, courtyard, portal and gallery into the fantasy of an Indian Palace in 1928.

All the guests were treated to a welcoming by an actual life-sized elephant. This elephant was a 6 stage process. Stage 1: a sculptor did "Royal Pindy," as the elephant came to be known, in clay. Eleanor went to Mexico with our dear friend and famous artist Helene Pfeffer to approve it. Stage 2: it was then moved on the flatbed it had been sculpted on, to the man who was to make the fiberglass mould. Stage 3: when this was finished, it went on a flatbed to the artist who painted it. Stage 4: it was then sent on a flatbed to the man who cut it into sections and built a steel armature which would be fitted inside the elephant to make it resistant to the often wild winds of New Mexico. Stage 5: it was shipped in a huge truck from Mexico to Santa Fe in 8 pieces. Stage 6: the final step, Eleanor brought two craftsmen from Mexico to place the elephant and join the armature for this magnificent creature. It is still here as a beacon and we love it as we drive in or out of our driveway. Everyone said it was the best party they had ever been to. This party was truly a *tour de force*.

The male part of the 58 in staff wore turbans, which our dear friend Birgit Zorniger brought from India and personally wrapped on every head. Patty's halter gown was in a wonderful bias pattern of blues, greens and mauves, and she was beautiful. Tony wore a fabulous Maharaja's jacket and pants with a blue bejeweled turban. Mark looked like an elegant Maharaja and Jake and his friend Desmond were dressed as young Maharajas. Alex and Max were dressed in the formal polo clothes of young Indian princes. Maddie was a glamorous Maharani and her sister Kathy was a siren in a slinky hot pink jeweled sari. Eleanor had taken a very old silver embroidered sari and designed a fantasy gown befitting the Duchess of Brenner. Of course it was black tie—a la 1928 India!

The Royals: Matilde the Duchess of Seville, Richard the Buke of Brenner, Jaggit the Maharajah of Jodphur, Eleanor the Duchess of Brenner, Benazir Maharanee of Tonk, Ganga Singh Maharajah of Bikaner, and the Princess.

Princess Jahan, Inderpal Prince of Jodphur, Viviaan Prince of Bikaner, Jumma Prince of Jodphur, Faaris Prince of Bikaner, and Lady Laeene of Kent

Ganga Singh the Maharajah of Bikaner with
Eleanor the Duchess of Brenner

Eleanor the Duchess of Brenner
with Matilde the Duchess of Seville

Sashi the Maharanee of Jath, Richard the Duke of Brenner,
Eleanor the Duchess of Brenner, and Lady Portia Vasano

The six tents in the courtyard were draped with thousands of yards of Indian silk in every hot color, the table cloths were hot pink, purple and orange, and the enormous ruby red stemware glittered in the thousands of tiny lights from the tent roofs. If you weren't there, you missed the grandest and most glamorous party Santa Fe has ever known and if you were there you know it was an evening to savor and never forget.

OUR 50ᵗʰ WEDDING ANNIVERSARY PARTY

I must add one party that Eleanor and I joyously attended but one we certainly did not orchestrate.

When our dear friend Robin Rubel discovered that we were to be officially married for 50 years on the 19ᵗʰ of December, 2006, she went to work. Her "two associates" were Sherry Ferguson and Donna Hankinson, also very dear and special friends of ours.

Robin knew that I very much enjoy Las Vegas and probably the gambling aspect, so she planned a Vegas extravaganza. It was a long weekend that started on Wednesday and ended on Sunday. The party itself took place on Friday evening, the 8ᵗʰ of December, 2006.

Robin chose the Okado Restaurant in the Wynn Hotel. The chef is Masa Ishizawa, who is world renowned and for good reason. The restaurant is surrounded by a coursing waterfall, lush gardens and a koi-filled lagoon. Robin pulled out all the stops. She and her team worked diligently with the Wynn's banquet manager. The chairs they chose were gold, the tables were decorated with gold runners, red and gold origami placecard holders, gold-tipped crystal, gold plates, and gold flatware. There were masses of orchids everywhere. It was truly magical. Eleanor was in heaven.

It was one of the most exquisite settings ever created for a party. Robin thought of everything, including a rare wine with gold flakes. There were 37 people attending (as that was all the room could hold). Robin had an exquisite book made with photographs of our extended family and very dear friends, all of whom wrote a special letter or tribute to us. Special people who attended the party were Jane and John Bagwell, Judy and Robert Block, Glenna and Curtis Boyd, Anthony Brenner and Maddie Schryer, Sarah and Doug Brown, Dianne and Don Chalmers, Terri and Alfy D'Ancona, Sherry and John Ferguson, Natalie Fitz-Gerald, Donna and Hal Hankinson, Patricia and Mark Jackson, Marci and Denny McLarry, Heidi and Chris McLarry, Beth and Steve Moise, Sandy and Russ Osterman, Robin and John Rubel, Kyla and Roger Thompson, Louise and Steve Tolber, and the guests of honor, the Duke and Duchess of Brenner. Listed above is Maddie Schryer who has been Tony's significant other for about six years. She is intelligent, charming, great looking and has a big heart and we have grown to love her very much.

The evening was perfection and will long live in our memories, not only for how wonderful our 50th anniversary was, but mostly because we know how truly blessed we have been.

For the spring and summer of 2010, Eleanor has four events planned: 1) the March joint birthday party of the Matteuccis and herself (Nedra is sixty, Richard sixty-five and Eleanor seventy-four); 2) John Rubel's 90th formal birthday party for 73 people, which will probably be one of the grandest parties we have ever given; 3) a fundraising dinner for Diane Denish who is currently the lieutenant governor of the State of New Mexico and who is running for governor, and 4) a major cocktail party, for 150, as a fundraiser for First Serve – New Mexico, the tennis and academic non-profit that we created and run, which will be discussed later in detail. In addition, we hosted a black-tie dinner for Bill Zeckendorf's 80th birthday, another black-tie dinner party for Valentine's Eve and a party for 200 for our dear friend Natalie Fitz-Gerald's 60th birthday. If it sounds like a lot, it is, especially with the general economy. I am the only person I know who has up-sized. All my friends are down-sizing.

MY GRANDCHILDREN

I want to state unequivocally that the greatest relationship is that between grandparents and grandchildren. It is a relationship that both the grandparents and grandchildren benefit from. There are no losers! I have been blessed with terrific grandchildren who are a pleasure to be around.

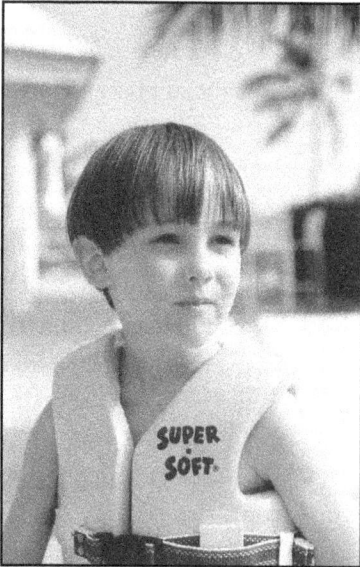

Christopher Pearce Jackson: 5 years old

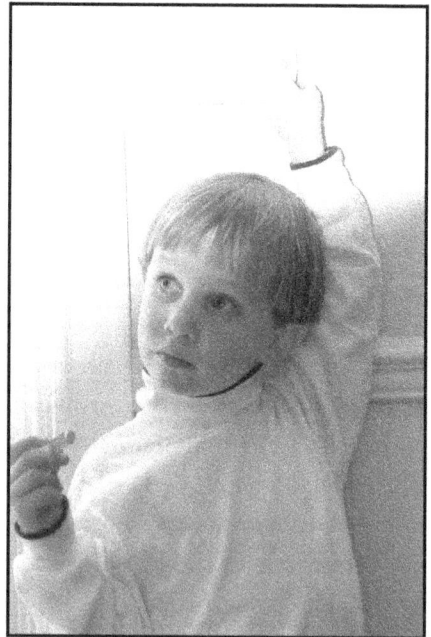

Jacob Brenner Jackson: 3 years old

First there are the Jackson children, Christopher and Jacob. As I write this in 2010, Christopher is 19 years old. He is severely autistic and lives at the Boston Hagashi School in Randolph, MA, near Boston, where he can live until he is 22 years old. He will never be able to live alone or without 24-hour supervision. His condition is a great sadness in our lives and extraordinarily difficult for his parents, Patty and Mark, and his brother, Jake, who are truly wonderful with him. Patty and Mark spend a lot of time flying from San Francisco to Boston every month and make his time at the school more fun and exciting, not to mention all the trips they plan with Chris when he is with them in San Anselmo on his home visits.

Chris and Mark

Christopher's father, Mark Jackson, is working diligently to organize a group facility called Sweetwater Spectrum for autistic young adults, both men and women, consisting of four separate residences, each accommodating four autistic adults for a center with 16 inhabitants. Of the 16 residents, 8 will be on scholarship. The facility will have a large playing field so that they can work off some of their energy. It will be located in Northern California, in Sonoma. Mark has committed himself to all aspects of the project, including developing the concept, meeting on prospective sites, and determining a budget. Very extensive fundraising must be undertaken to achieve his goal. It is a grand and much needed undertaking and I wish him well. Mark has contributed four years of his life to the project, as has Patty, who is in charge of the capital campaign. They have personally contributed a sizeable sum of money as well. Today, one out of every hundred children is autistic. What an incredible project Mark is doing. Hopefully, it will be a pilot for many other communities for the autistic young adults of America.

Crazy Hair Day with the Cousins

The Cousins: Jake, Alex, Chris, and Max

Alex, Tony, Maddie, and Max at Jake's Bar Mitzvah

The Cousins: Max, Jake, and Alex

The very proud Grandy and Tai Tai with Jake

The Wonderful Jacksons

Christopher's brother, Jacob Brenner Jackson (Jake), was Bar Mitzvahed four years ago and is now 17 years old. He did a superb job at his Bar Mitzvah and we were all tremendously proud of him. He attends the Marin School in Marin, CA, and is the only ninth and tenth grader to qualify for the outstanding scholastic honors group with straight A's. He is also a master of an action game called laser tag, located in San Diego, where the people are divided into two teams battling against each other in a simulated war using laser guns as their weapons. Mark is his avid partner in this unusual father-son activity.

Tony's sons are Alexander and Maxwell (Alex and Max) and they are well known in Santa Fe, since they spend a great deal of time with us. They live in San Francisco and have an easy trip to visit us. The house really lights up, as do we, when they are here with their wonderful sense of humor and personalities. Max and Alex both earn straight A's or A-'s in school. Max, 13 years old, was Bar Mitzvahed on March 17th, 2010, and his brother, Alex, two years earlier. Both boys did an excellent job.

Max is a fine athlete, specializing in basketball and tennis, and has 150 girls as his friends on Facebook. (Need I say more?) Alex knows what he wants to do and is very focused and goal-oriented. Alexander is 16 years old and a sophomore in high school. He already has set his sights on a career in real estate and was responsible for finding Tony's new house on Broadway in San Francisco. He tracked home listings on his computer and insisted that Tony visit the house which Tony ended up buying. Now Alex is concentrating on his tennis and has a goal of becoming a Division 1 college tennis player. He is currently co-president of Branson High School's tenth grade and is busy planning events for his class.

Alexander Julian Brenner: 5 years old

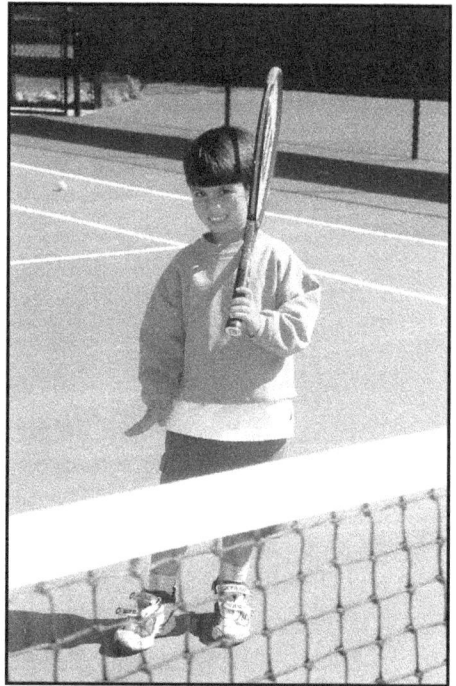

Maxwell Tucker Brenner: 5 years old

From Grandfather to Father to Son: Alexander's Bar Mitzvah

Great joy for Grandy and Tai Tai with their Alexander

Three Generations of Brenner Men

The family at Maxwell Tucker Brenner's Bar Mitzvah

A Divine Blessing

As mentioned, at an early age I introduced Max and Alex to tennis, and they have developed into good players. I arrange lessons and matches for them when they are in Santa Fe. In fact, Alex called me a year ago, and said he would like to play tennis at a Division 1 college but would need coaching, playing time and travelling time to tournaments for himself and his coach. Alex asked if I would sponsor him with the coach of his choice and financially support his coaching, tournaments, and travel. I asked him to let me think about it and get back to him with my decision. We had many subsequent conversations and when I was in San Francisco I met Hubert, who is the coach Alex chose. I finally agreed as I felt that Alex would be very dedicated to his tennis goals and that he had thought deeply about his choice. Hubert has been an immense influence on Alex and is fanatic about physical conditioning, footwork, serving technique and all the little corrections that contribute to tennis performance. Alex claims his serve is now 110 MPH and in the summer of 2010 was busy playing pressure tennis (tournaments). I asked Alex how he liked his coach and he said, "He's great, I really love him." In spring and summer of 2010 he played in USTA local California tournaments as well as national events, so it is our loss that he was in Santa Fe for only one week during the summer. As a freshman in high school at Branson, Alex played number one on their varsity tennis team and is playing number one again this year. I'm vicariously living tennis once again and I am thrilled with his progress. However, with my sponsorship comes advice: *When you have someone on the ropes finish them off, do not let up. Be mentally tough and analyze your opponent's vulnerability. You have to have total focus and concentration. In a tough match hang in there because a lot of players cannot sustain that level of effort. And most importantly, have fun.* The boys have benefitted greatly from the instructions they have received from Timothy Garcia, a judge in the New Mexico appeals court. Tim played on the circuit for a few years and is on the nominating committee of the USTA as well as in the New Mexico Hall of Fame. He has graciously shared his knowledge, skill and experience with Alex and Max, and they just think he is wonderful. Tim, his beautiful wife Nancy, and their marvelous children Amy and Ted have become wonderful members of our extended family.

OUR DOGS

In all our married life, Eleanor and I had never owned a dog—except when Tony brought a dog home as a seventh grader. Where he found this dog I do not remember, but I forced him to choose between his father and the dog since I was allergic to dogs at that time. Tony loves dogs, so it was a tough choice!

In 1999 in Santa Fe, it seemed as though every family had at least one dog and many had two or three. We joined the Westminster Kennel Club and ordered a female Rhodesian ridgeback from a breeder on Long Island. Rhodesian ridgebacks are dogs native to Rhodesia who were bred and trained to hunt African lions. They are usually very brave and athletic and run and jump amazingly. I remember one day when one of our Rhodesians jumped a five-foot wall and also at another time jumped from the ground through the open window of my car. They also have selective hearing. If you whisper "treat" or "food" they come immediately, but if you call them to come without incentives they merely look at you and lie down. Very sweet-natured dogs and not very demanding, they like their space and love to lie in the sun. Our first dog was named Lady. Before we picked her up from the breeder we had to build a kennel adjacent to the house. In addition, we felt we needed an invisible fence around the house and part of our property so that Lady could run loose. In theory this invisible fence would keep her from crossing the electric current. In reality, she would race across the electrically charged fence whenever she wanted to. Maybe this type of fence works for other dogs, but if Lady wanted out she just ran right through it. We called Lady the $10,000 dog (and this was just the beginning) after we paid for the kennel, the invisible fence, and substantial medical bills when she broke her leg racing alongside a truck at six months old. The break was very serious, as it was very close to her growth plate, so it took a long time and many vet bills to heal. Lady was a sweet, elegant dog with innate intelligence. She was our first dog so we spoiled her in a major way. She loved to ride in the car and we often took her with us for drives. We met the breeder, Mary, at the airport in New York City, to pick up Lady when she was eight weeks old. We transported her in a Sherpa bag and put her under the plane seat. She was a little angel, only peering out once or twice on the trip home. Lady was difficult to train. She had bowel movements ten to twelve times a day anywhere she felt the need—but finally she became a wonderful pet who was well known throughout our neighborhood. She was very friendly with our neighbors' two dogs and when they moved away we thought she

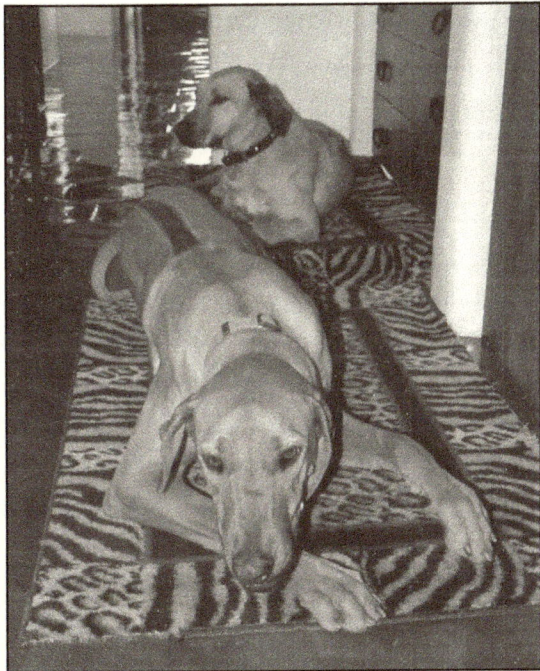

Lady and Kelly: 2008

181

needed a companion. We ordered another female ridgeback from a breeder in California from whom our daughter, Patricia, had purchased her male ridgeback. (Ridgebacks run in the family.) Along came Kelly, who was shipped in a crate on an airplane from San Francisco. We took Kelly home and it was late at night. As I opened the door to the house she raced past me, but not having ever been there before, she flew over the staircase to the guest house and landed on the floor 19 steps below, fortunately without injury. Lady and Kelly became great friends and got along famously.

We enjoyed both dogs tremendously. Lady for nearly nine years and Kelly for five and counting. It was a very sad day when we discovered that Lady had very aggressive cancer of the leg. She had been hospitalized with cancer previously and had spent 15 days in the hospitals in Santa Fe and Albuquerque. All the doctors felt Lady had totally beaten cancer. This time, the vet said, "This particular cancer, which attacks big dogs, is terminal." Lady died several months later, but we were happy to have had her for the time we did. We buried her on our property in a proper grave in the land she loved. We miss her, but the other dogs keep us busy. All I can say is that Lady and the others, Kelly and Midas, our royal standard poodle, have enriched our lives and have contributed to our happiness in Santa Fe.

Knowing that Lady was to die, we once gain felt we needed a companion dog, this time for Kelly. A friend of ours, Karen Herhahn, had three white poodles, all well behaved. Karen found a rescue facility in Colorado and we drove there to see and pick up a poodle. The rescue woman assured us the dog was house broken and trained. It could not have been further from the truth. She also told us Midas was two and a half years old and a royal standard poodle. The only true statement was his size: a royal standard. We soon discovered that Midas must have been abused, as he was a very nervous and hyper dog. The rescue people in Colorado offered to take him back, but Eleanor had fallen in love with him and could not part with him. Midas is a cocoa-colored poodle and very big. He is a male dog and constantly in trouble, so we call him "Marley" after the dog in the movie. In the movie Marley is a terrible puppy, and he stayed that way as he grew up, but his people stuck with him and ended up loving him. We now say to Midas, "You are our Marley."

Midas Brenner

So, there we were with three dogs for several months! Eleanor loves Midas, who is very affectionate and needy, and I would be happy if Marley were somewhere else. Not really! Even I have become attached to him.

FIRST SERVE – NEW MEXICO
OUR NON-PROFIT

Eleanor and I formed First Serve – New Mexico in 2003 as a way to give back to the children of our community and ultimately to America. Eleanor originally spent a year in the public school system working with young girls at risk. After this experience, she became very depressed and negative on what was NOT being accomplished in the public schools. We then asked ourselves, what would be the best way to make a major contribution to the future well-being of our Santa Fe kids. Eleanor came up with a concept and our mission statement, which clearly stated our goals and plan of action, but before we could tackle such an undertaking, we had to be sure we had the necessary start-up funds. We raised $125,000 in contributions of $25,000 each from ourselves, the United States Tennis Association (USTA), the McCune Foundation, the Andrew Davis Family, and the Life Center, which would be enough to fund the organization for the first two years. Alan Schwartz was at the time president of the USTA, and he was very encouraging on the formation of First Serve New Mexico since his focus was on bringing tennis into inner city locations. He helped facilitate the USTA grant.

Alan and Ronnie have been dear friends for over 50 years. Except for the Life Center, all of our initial contributors are still with us, which speaks to the fact that they have been very satisfied with our results. We started the program with 18 kids and two schools in the year 2003 and now have six schools and 100 kids. Eleanor is the motivating and driving force behind the program and is responsible for its success. I am the treasurer. She goes to school or works on First Serve-New Mexico just about five days a week. Eleanor is the role model for the program. It is an intense program but with great results.

To tell you more about the program (from our brochure):

First Serve – New Mexico is a four day per week, two hours per day, after-school program that reinforces the belief that total commitment and hard work leads to success. The unique combination of intensive academic tutoring twice a week and intensive tennis instruction is motivating New Mexico students to become actively engaged in their own success and to form long term friendships with other members of First Serve.

It is the vision of First Serve – New Mexico to prevent or cure the problem of student disengagement in its earliest stages. The program is designed to encourage students to dream, and we provide them the tools to put their dreams into action.

First Serve – New Mexico is a school-based program where all of the tutors are licensed teachers and tennis instruction is provided by professional coaches. When the child is ready and proficient in all their strokes and serving, they are entered into tournaments to compete with tennis players throughout the State of New Mexico.

First Serve – New Mexico is a structured two-hour a day, four-day a week after-school tutoring and tennis instruction program, two days in tutoring and two days in tennis. The tutoring is tailored to the academic needs of each individual student, and administered by licensed teachers. Core groups are created with 4-8 students, one tutor and one tennis instructor. Each school has a licensed teacher who serves as the school coordinator and is responsible for tracking each student through the program so that issues are identified early and negative trends can be reversed. This is hands-on, labor-intensive, child-centered approach which allows for the development of strong bonds and real knowledge of each participating child's individual challenges.

First Serve's innovative approach is to be totally accountable to the progress of each and every participating student. This is the only after-school program in the state with 100% accountability.

The program uses a comprehensive tracking tool to measure quarterly progress towards the objectives of self-discipline, scholastic expertise, tennis proficiency, self-confidence and self-esteem. Grades, standardized testing scores and commentaries from tutors, teachers, coordinators, tennis coaches, parents and the students themselves help identify specific areas of focus to ensure that each student becomes the very best they can be.

First Serve – New Mexico has a wonderful program director, Elizabeth Chisholm. Elizabeth has worked with Eleanor for five years. Miranda Katko is the terrific head coordinator for the schools, and has worked with Eleanor for two years. Maddie Pack has been the head coach for First Serve – New Mexico since its inception. She has been an unbelievable mentor to all the children, developing talented and accredited tennis players who, with time and effort, can become fine tennis players. First Serve – New Mexico has an interstate tournament team that the USTA invites to play in other states in the southwest region.

The program works! We know that we have dramatically changed the lives of at least 150 children for the better plus the uncountable ripple effect.

First Serve – New Mexico is a passion for Eleanor and me. We fervently believe that superb education and expertise in an individual sport, along with deep caring from adults and strong and totally positive peer friendships will help to not only enhance the lives of these children but most importantly set these students on a path to great successes for themselves and for our country. First Serve – New Mexico is blessed to have a most involved and remarkable board. As of this date, we have 17 members on the board. Each and every one of our board is not only extraordinarily outstanding personally and career-wise, but also totally dedicated to the children of First Serve – New Mexico. They are very special. Not only are we blessed to have dear and wonderful friends on this board but most importantly are the children of First Serve – New Mexico. In alphabetical order:

Eleanor P. Brenner, President
Richard A. Brenner, Treasurer
Jeannine Daniels
Diane Doniger
Sherry Ferguson
Cherie Gamble
Donna Hankinson
Karen Herhahn
Sharon Loy
Mike McGonagle
Exilda Martinez, Secretary
Don D. Moya, Vice President
Russ Osterman
Mary C. Ross
Carolyn Schmidt
Margaret Steward
Jean Van Camp

SOME RANDOM THOUGHTS ON SANTA FE

Life in Santa Fe is at the other end of the spectrum from New York City. New York City has a frenetic energy, a stressful vitality and urgency. Santa Fe has a peaceful, sometimes slow-paced level of activity. When driving in Santa Fe, you rarely hear a horn blown, whereas in New York City there is a discordant chorus of noise from horns blowing in traffic, ambulances, police cars, sirens, alarms and on and on. People in cars in Santa Fe wait quietly and politely and will let you in a line, whereas in New York City you'd think you were trying to steal their child if you want to enter their traffic lane. When you're walking on the street, people naturally say good morning or give you a friendly and warm smile. In New York City if you are on a public bus or subway, look at the people's faces and see how stressed they are.

I must admit that when I first came to Santa Fe, it was a big adjustment. Eleanor says I do not like change, whether it's old clothes or old places. It took me about six months to acclimate myself and to become really comfortable with the different pace of Santa Fe. Now I love it and can think of no place in the world that I would rather live. (More about this later.)

Santa Fe is a small city, but the people who live here are the most giving, charitable people that I have ever known. There are probably more non-profits here than in much larger cities, with participants who give not only money but also the time commitment necessary to make the organization succeed. Then there are our very dear friends and fishing buddies, Dianne & Don Chalmers. Don is the most supportive guy in New Mexico philanthropy and he always makes sure that First Serve-New Mexico meets its annual financial goal. It is really extraordinary. Another thing I was not prepared for was the State of New Mexico itself. The state is, physically, very large but it has a population of less than 2.1 million people, so there is a great deal of open space. The state ranks very poorly in many critical areas, like the percentage of kids who finish high school, teenage pregnancy, educational levels, drunken driving, gun shot fatalities and on and on. Needless to say, Santa Fe is in many ways an anomaly compared to the rest of the state. With this smallness comes a relationship with so many different people that in your ordinary life, in a big city, you would not have. For example, you really know your congressman, Ben Ray Lujan, your senator, Tom Udall, and your governor, and they know you. You see them at local functions for non-profits, at basketball games and on and on. You can be a mover and shaker yourself, a "big frog in a little pond." As I explained previously, Tano Norte was originally a dirt road, but working through Ben Lujan, the speaker of the state house of representatives, who has become a good friend, I was able to present to a committee of the state legislature a case for paving the road. I called Tom Udall several years ago and asked him if he would draw the winning raffle ticket for our First Serve fundraiser, which he did. Your friends can encompass a vast range of people, from physicists at Los Alamos National Laboratories to world-renowned plastic surgeons, and from gallery owners and artists to presidents of colleges. One gallery owner is Chris McLarry. He and his beautiful wife Heidi have been part of our extended family for more years than I can believe. I feel very good about Chris since I had advised him on the opening of his first successful gallery in Santa Fe called McLarry Fine Arts. He now has two galleries. I also was instrumental in the formation of the very successful Bodywise Physical Therapy Company.

Heather Robertson and the late Suzy Gershon have helped me greatly in retaining good health.

Our friends are amazing. We are so grateful to them and for them.

SURGERY AND BACK PROBLEMS

Since I have been in Santa Fe, I have suffered with serious back and neck problems and have had eight surgeries, none of which completely alleviated the pain. From 2005 to September of 2007 I had a very debilitating nerve pain from my right knee to right hip, requiring me to use a cane and to limit the time I spent walking or standing. In 2004 and 2005, the pain was so constant and debilitating that Hal Hankinson referred me to two spine specialists in New York City. One was from Columbia Presbyterian, and other from the Hospital for Special Surgery; both were head of the spine departments at their respective institutions. They both were to paint a very bleak picture, indicating that they would have to operate from the front and the back and the operation would take a minimum of eleven hours, and that there was a substantial risk of morbidity and that I would need additional surgery beyond this. The doctor at Presbyterian said he would not recommend operating.

In September of 2007 I was scheduled for surgery with an American of East-Indian heritage, Sanjay Khourana. He is a brilliant young orthopedist of 37 years in age, who is handsome and charming as well as very nice. I was introduced to him through a friend from Las Campanas, Gary Kramer, who had a problem similar to mine (but much more straightforward, and without all my complications). Gary's surgery was very successful and I spoke to my very close friend and neurosurgeon, Hal Hankinson, about doing the same operation. Hal thought the operation might work and that Sanjay might help me. I had to send Dr. Khourana current CAT scans and x-rays and an old MRI for him to examine before he would even see me.

I saw Dr. Khourana at his office in Marina Del Rey, fifteen minutes from the LAX airport, in August 2007, and he explained the novel, revolutionary new procedure he had helped to perfect. It is done on an operating table that is flat and converts to convex, thereby stretching out your spine and opening up the spaces between your vertebrae. Dr. Khourana planned to insert one wedge at the trouble point in my spine and another where he would take out part of a rib in order to release the pinched nerves. However, when I came back for the surgery on September 18, he had changed his opinion and was only going to insert one wedge in the area of my rib. He said, "If you were my father, what I propose to do for you is what I would do for him." This is exactly what he did. Dr. Khourana's surgery took less than two hours, as compared to the New York doctors' estimates of 11 to 14 hours. He had to break a rib to place the wedge in position, but I was able to leave the hospital two days after the operation. I had to be very careful for several months to allow the wedge to fuse to the spine. This takes fully six months and is not completely fused for about a year. The operation was successful beyond comprehension. The wedge released the nerve pain as hoped, and I can now walk and stand for a significant length of time. I am even able to play a little tennis again, which I love. It really was amazing and I have recommended many new patients to him with similar great results. It just proves that you should never give up and keep your eyes and ears open for new and different approaches. Bless Dr. Khourana's talent and may he continue to help people like me for many years.

OIL AND GAS INVESTING WITH JOHN RUBEL

I started investing in oil and gas stocks in 2002, believing this would offer me great future potential for investment appreciation. In 2003, when John Rubel and I started working together, I was somewhat incapacitated because of a recent surgery and John worked the computer program for me. We started looking at small oil stocks that paid a dividend, like Enerplus Resources and San Juan Basic Royalty Trust, and then John discovered the Canadian Oil Sands Trust. We subsequently took a big position in this company and have made considerable profit in that investment. We probably know more about Canadian Oil Sands in Alberta, Canada than most other investors. We still believe in it, but there are environmental drawbacks that we have had to give serious consideration. It was a great learning experience, with each step leading us further into some limited expertise in the field of oil and gas. John is a brilliant man and as nice as he is intelligent. He has a flair and desire for as thorough knowledge as he can possibly obtain, and he would do in-depth and exceptionally thorough research and analysis on specific matters that we would be thinking about. I was more intuitive

193

and instinctive in approach, and between us the combination worked very well. We would each reach our own conclusions and act accordingly, repeatedly reviewing these same decisions to see if the situation had changed, calling for a different investment approach. Today, unlike 20 years ago, you cannot simply make an investment and hold it. You must constantly review your investments and be open to changing your positions, switching your portfolio or eliminating your position entirely. You must be flexible in your approach and be as objective as possible. You must not fall in love with your own ideas. At the same time, you must give your investment decisions time to work and not churn your account unnecessarily. "Churning" means too much buying and selling. This benefits the broker but disadvantages the client.

John and I did very nicely, with excellent results, but we were so focused on oil and gas that we did not see the bubble coming in the mortgage-backed securities, caused by credit default swaps and collateralized debt obligations (CDOs) of no-value sub-prime mortgages. The whole banking and real estate industries were devastated and barely survived. In the United States and throughout most of the world, a tremendous amount of wealth was destroyed. Except a rarified few, everyone was badly hurt in the 2008 chaos that occurred in the stock market when the Dow Jones average fell from 14,000 to well below 7,000. We still are in oil and gas and believe that it is still the most exciting and potentially rewarding sector for us to be investing in. We will see, but it's been great fun working with John.

I will mention some of the conclusions and opinions that we have derived from studying the economics of oil and natural gas.

1.   The world is facing increasing long term demand for crude oil, with impressive growth in developing countries such as India, China and the rest of Asia.

2.   The world's supply of easily reachable crude oil is diminishing at a rate of about 6-8% per year with many of the lower-cost, major well locations having decreased productivity. Some examples of the decreased production from the giant fields are: the Mexican

fields, the North Sea fields and even the giant Saudia Arabia fields.

3. The deep-water wells that have recently been discovered in Brazil and shown to have plentiful quantities of oil are very deep in the ocean. Some are one mile or more in depth, and then it is necessary to drill below the ocean floor another three to four miles to reach the oil, all of this in treacherous water. Drilling is done from platforms and these platforms are very costly to operate, running in excess of $500,000 a day. As an example, British Petroleum had a blow out of a well off the coast of Louisiana, resulting in one of the greatest environmental disasters of all time. The entire seafood industry of Louisiana was shut down for an extended period and untold environmental damage was done to the Gulf region.

4. Based on supply and demand and the lack of a viable substitute, the price of oil should rise dramatically over the long term.

5. Transportation will continue to mainly use oil and gas as its fuel of choice and necessity for a long time to come.

6. Alternative fuels will be difficult and very time-consuming to develop. Many will be like ethanol, which was a momentary flash, quick to subside because corn-based ethanol is not economically feasible. It takes more energy to grow, process and transport it than it yields as a fuel. Moreover, using corn as its base source material causes corn prices to rise, increasing the cost for feed and fuel. This is exacerbated by the need to devote more acreage to food production. Another problem is that many states have passed laws requiring ethanol to be sold in their state, resulting in higher-priced ethanol being sold in the U.S. instead of less expensive sugar-cane ethanol that could be imported from Brazil. Because sugar-cane is five to six times richer than corn, ethanol production in Brazil is far more cost-effective than in the U.S.

7. The most viable alternate fuel may be fuel cells or batteries, but the

path for this industry will be long and rocky with developmental and logistical problems.

8. There may also be a big opportunity in natural gas, since it is plentiful and much cheaper than oil to drill for. However, natural gas has problems as well. These include the high cost of drilling in numerous sites, the pollution of ground waters, the lack of retail facilities to store and sell natural gas, and the lack of adequate interconnected pipelines. The pollution aspect, I do believe, is much more serious than has been heretofore determined. The leaking takes place in the process of collecting the gas, when the pollutants slip through the ground and into the ground water. Exxon Mobil has recently purchased at a substantial premium, XTO, a major natural gas driller and producer. This is important because Exxon is, far and away, the leading producer of energy in the world. If Exxon validates a technology, the entire industry often follows.

For all reasons, we made a huge bet in the oil industry. Even with the market collapse of 2008 – 2009, we had still increased our portfolio substantially since 2002.

Eleanor and the Duke at lunch in the member's club private dining room:
Wimbledon, 2003

THE TRIP OF A LIFETIME
AFRICA 2002

Our trip to Africa in 2002 was the greatest trip we have ever taken, truly a once in a lifetime adventure. As I reflect on the trip, it seems to have been perfection. On April 19th 2002, we departed from Santa Fe and flew to Frankfurt and then on to Berlin where we stayed at the Four Seasons Hotel. We did a great deal of sightseeing in Berlin, visiting the Reichstag, the Jewish Museum designed by Daniel Liebeskind, the National Museums, and many other cultural and historical sites. A word about the Jewish Museum. After spending 90 minutes there, we were very solemn, sad and quiet, each thinking about what we had seen and how deeply we were affected.

At the time of our visit, there seemed to be new construction on every corner in East Berlin. We attended two fine performances of the Berlin Symphony and visited the old symphony hall, which was built to house 32,000 people. It was later used as Gestapo headquarters, and from this location the deportation of millions of Jews and others was orchestrated. From music and its beauty to a planning point for the Holocaust. Catastrophic!

Leaving Johannesburg for Botswana

On the 25th of April, we left for Johannesburg and stayed at the beautiful and charming Saxon Hotel. This is where Eleanor discovered Rooibos tea, which became her new favorite tea and which she drank throughout Africa. The following day we flew in a small plane to Jao, the first of four safaris and game reserves that we were to experience. At Jao we stayed in a room measuring 13 feet wide by 50 feet long with a thatched roof. It was totally surrounded by dramatic Marula trees (native to this area), palm trees, birds and animals. We went on safari twice a day, early evening and early morning. The wine and food was great and in the evenings we ate on our private terrace and watched the rising of the full African moon. The camps we visited were the height of luxury and elegance with unbelievable service.

On our first night in Jao we went on safari in a Range Rover and saw hippopotamus, weighing 3,500 to 7,000 pounds. African buffalos are the most dangerous animal in Africa, even more so than hippos, though hippos are responsible for the most human deaths. It was sunset on the safari and we stopped for wine and hors d'oeuvres out in the bush, not 30 yards away from a herd of elephants. We did not bother them and they did not bother us. We spent a few days seeing all the animals: cheetahs, giraffes, lions, etc. One day the Range Rover was charged by a white rhino, and the driver shot off his rifle to prevent us from being hit. The first night's dinner on our own private terrace was so special we continued to do so, with separate servers, great food and wine, and beautiful nights. What could be more romantic?

On April 28th we went back to the airstrip for a seven-minute flight to Little Mambo, in Botswana, where the staff of 35 sang a welcome song to us upon our arrival. Little Mambo had a total of three guest tents for six people only. We, however, were the only guests. We were cautioned on arrival about being very careful and only coming and going to our tent with a rifle-armed guide. We continued our private dinners and in the morning, when we awoke, we viewed Cape buffalo that had come in under our tent and into our backyard. Little Mambo is located on a vast reserve called the Murelli Reserve. Here too we had twice-a-day safaris and wonderful food and saw all the possible animals we could wish for, from leopards to lions to elephants to cheetahs to giraffes and on and on. Eleanor was jumping for joy.

On April 30th, we departed Mambo and flew to the city of Kensane in Zimbabwe, where we stayed at the Stanley and Livingston Hotel. The ten-room Stanley and Livingston Hotel was similar to an elegant British country lodge. The entire staff was black. We ate dinner in the hotel restaurant where we had the company of one other couple for our first evening and otherwise had the place all to ourselves. That afternoon we went for a boat ride on the Zambezi River in a flat-bottomed boat. We were the only passengers, as this romantic sojourn had been orchestrated by our incredible South African travel agent, Jocelyn Miller. The Zambezi is huge and is the fourth largest river in Africa. From the boat we saw elephants, hippos and gigantic crocodiles, about eight to ten feet in length. On the boat we were offered hors d'oeuvres and wine. The next morning we were off to the elephant camp, where Eleanor rode on an elephant for the entire morning—great fun! She always wanted this experience. I tried, but could not spread my legs wide enough to be comfortable because of my hip replacements.

Then on to our big adventure, which we call the "hippo incident." Our travel agent Jocelyn Miller found a handsome, 6'2" guide, Paul Connery, who was famous in this area because he had once fought a leopard with his bare hands in his kitchen until a neighbor came to his rescue and shot the leopard. He was featured in National Geographic magazine. According to his instructions, which had started with Eleanor's requests, Paul was to find and arrange, on a small island in the Zambezi River, a romantic lunch with champagne in a silver bucket, fine food, a table with a white linen cloth, beautiful china, and no other people. This Hollywood movie set was no easy task. However, to reach this island you first had to canoe from the shore. Paul put us into the canoe and had a lookout man in a second canoe to warn us of any problems (I should have asked why). We were about three-quarters of the way to the island when the lookout warned him that a giant, male hippo obviously felt threatened that we had violated his territory. (Hippos are exceptionally territorial.) He charged at us through the water with his mouth wide open—it looked like a deep cavern—bellowing at the top of his lungs. The speed at which he was charging at us was astounding. The guide was frantic but he maintained his calm. He later told us that because we were in a becalmed area, he had no choice but to paddle towards the hippo, cutting down the distance that separated us from the island. As he furiously paddled towards the island, terrifyingly, only 10 yards separated us from the hippo. We reached the island just before the hippo reached us. Our guide yanked us out of the canoe and shouted at us to run up the hill because he thought the hippo was so enraged he might charge out of the water. Later, over a romantic lunch with all the accoutrements, while the hippo was still bellowing and waiting for us to return, Paul told us this was the closest call he'd ever had as a guide on the Zambezi. When it was time to leave and the hippo was still bellowing, I told him he had to find another way home. He and the lookout carried the canoes across the island and we returned safely from the Hippopotamus Incident by canoe, taking a different direction to avoid the hippo. Eleanor's only comment after this was that I should have taken pictures. Mine was the thought that we had come all that way to die in Africa.

We also visited Zimbabwe to see Victoria Falls, one of the natural wonders of the world. The falls extend over a very wide area and come crashing down the mountains. It is a most majestic and overpowering sight. One that we will never forget.

A little background on Zimbabwe. Zimbabwe had been called Rhodesia when it was under British rule. Rhodesia had been the breadbasket for its own country and great parts of southern Africa. Now all the land, of which 90 percent previously had been owned and cultivated by white Rhodesian farmers, has been annexed and confiscated by Robert Mugabe. He turned it over to black Africans in small parcels. The people do not have the desire, know-how or education to manage the land. Most of the people, quite sadly, are illiterate and unable to function except on a very basic level. The farms and ranches are not operating on any productive level and the people are pathetically poor with inadequate food, housing, and water. No longer are the farms productive. Now Zimbabwe must import basic food products from other countries. An adequate amount of food for good health is not provided. If you stop to shop at an outdoor market you are accosted by 30 or 40 people begging for money. There is massive unemployment, running to over 90 percent of the population. Zimbabwe is a beautiful country with great natural resources, but with an inept and cruel dictator it portends to total failure for the majority of its citizens. We were very happy to leave Zimbabwe.

On May 2nd we flew from Zimbabwe to Cape Town. Arriving by plane, you can see how beautiful the city is. We stayed at the Ellerman House. We had an unbelievable suite, one of only eleven suites that comprise the hotel. There were only six guests when we arrived. Cape Town is a great city and we had an excellent driver who showed us all the sites of the city and surrounding areas, going as far as the mountains in the north and in the south to the tip of Africa, the Cape of Good Hope. On the way to the Cape of Good Hope we passed a section of about 200 yards where the street was lined with monkeys. Thousands of monkeys were sitting on the curbs on both sides of the highway. The Cape of Good Hope is where the Indian Ocean, smooth and calm, meets the Atlantic, which has crushing waves with huge boulders and rocks. An enormous contrast and a really majestic site! Then back to Cape Town, shopping for baskets, masks, all kinds of goodies. The Holocaust Museum in Cape Town was amazing. Nelson Mandela was responsible for this being opened two years ago. It is required that all school children spend one and half hours going through the museum. It was pervasively very sad but it was uplifting to see that the school children were learning about what had occurred.

The Duke enjoying tea in our suite at The Ellerman House:
Capetown, South Africa 2002

We then went back to Johannesburg and met our African travel agent who had done such a fine job planning our trip. After lunch and warm goodbyes to Jocelyn and part of her staff, we left for Johannesburg for our last two safaris.

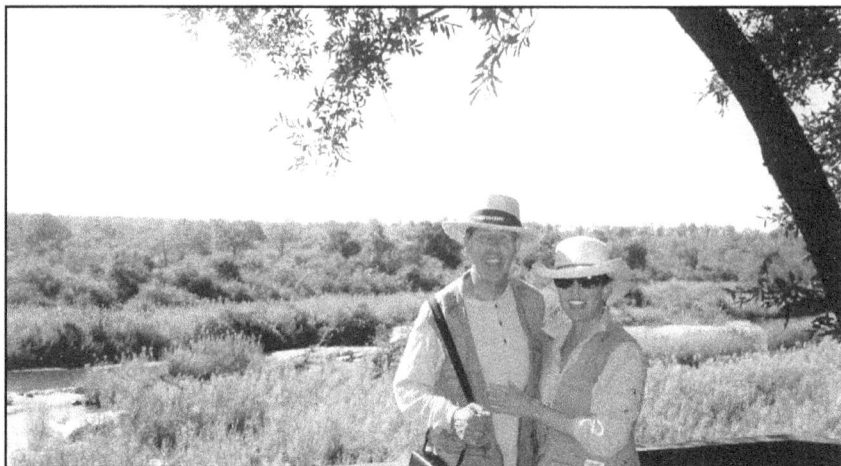

Eleanor and the Duke in the savanna at the Royal Malewane Lodge; the Bushveld at a private game preserve, South African 2002

Our first safari was The Royal Malewane Lodge, which housed a total of eight guests. We were the only guests after the first evening. The view was spectacular, looking across a waterway and seeing the animals parading by our location. There was a very large deck, which was 60 feet in length. We had cocktails there and looked across the waterway at the animals. This was a different kind of camp. It is situated in the heart of Africa's finest Bushveld on a private game reserve adjacent to the Kruger National Park. Again, each camp has a separate personality, approach, and a different ambiance. This camp was primarily a tracking camp where you were walking with a guide and an armed guard to see the animals more in their own habitat. It is home to Africa's Big Five: lion, leopard, elephant, African buffalo and rhinoceros.

The last camp we visited was Singita Boulders, which means The Miracle. All these camps are located on the range in South Africa. They pride themselves on luxurious accommodations and great service. There are 12 luxurious suites and they are quite elegant, with a private pool for each suite. The food is exquisite and the wines superb. The suite we occupied is the epitome of elegance and graciousness. The views of the savanna and the roaming animals are beyond belief. At last it was May 4th and we again returned to the small airstrip and then to the airport which was the first leg of our trip home. And thus ended perfection.

The Duke on Safari: Singita Boulders, Kruger Park, South Africa 2002

Richard the Duke of Brenner

Business-Related:

1. If it doesn't pass the smell test, don't force it. Meaning go with your instinct and be careful.
2. If it sounds too good to be true, beware, because it probably is not.
3. When people stop talking about you, that's the time to worry.
4. There is a right price for a product. Don't be blinded by the cost, but consider its intrinsic value as well.
5. When in doubt, leave it out.
6. Markdowns are like taking a high colonic: You feel better when it's over.
7. Your first markdown is your best markdown… make it deep and do it promptly.
8. A deal is a deal. (This is relative to Tony who sold his bike to Willie Galleson for $20.00 and Willie paid him $15.00. So, Tony was instructed by me to get the bike back or the $5.00.)
9. Do you have to make that decision now? If not, with time they often disappear.
10. Everyone puts on their pants one leg at a time. Think how silly people look sitting on the john.
11. A peacock today, a feather duster tomorrow.
12. You never lose money taking a profit.
13. Some things that seem like the worst often turn out to be the best, and vice versa.
14. All you have is your integrity. Your word is your bond.
15. Sometimes, the best deal is the one that you lost.

Life-Related:

1. People are consistent. Meaning the way they are to you is the way they are to others as well.
2. If it ain't broke, don't fix it.
3. Re dating: be like the Fifth Avenue bus which stops at every corner.
4. When do you stop being a father (or mother)? When they put you in the box.
5. People don't change. They are who they are.
6. Always let someone save face.
7. You can't be a little bit pregnant. You either are or not.
8. If you want something done, ask a busy person to do it.
9. It's not over until the fat lady sings.
10. You can never win an argument with a fool.
11. Rise and shine.
12. No one knows more than a high school senior and less than a college freshman.
13. Children grow up in spite of the parents, not because of them.
14. You learn more from your failures than your successes.
15. Who appointed you judge and juror?
16. Make the most of each day—it's a gift.
17. Being a parent is like shooting an arrow. Point them in the right direction, but let them fly solo.
18. After doing the best you can do and it is not working, it's time to walk away and say, "The hell with it."
19. If you don't stand up for yourself, then who will?
20. Do not worry until you have to. Be aware bad news travels fast. No news is good news.
21. If I won't tell you the truth, then who will?
22. The best is yet to come.

P eople ask me why I like Santa Fe. My answer is the sky, the mountains, and best of all the people. The sky is high and open and has many changing faces, from stormy grey to a magnificent vibrant blue. The clouds on a bright day look like cotton sculptures. On several days a year, the clouds come down to meet the mountains and hang very low over them, creating a surreal feeling. The mountains are majestic and changeable like a chameleon with the time of day and the nature of the weather. Right now they are very snowy and the skiers are very happy. When it snows the mountains become a winter wonderland and at other times, a hiker's fantasy, for there are many beautiful and great trails—some easy and some very difficult.

But the very best thing about Santa Fe, without doubt, is the people. We have been blessed to make such very wonderful friends. As our dear friend Don Chalmers says, "People in the west are warm and welcoming." Indeed they are! The friends we see the most are Beth and Steve Moise, Jeannine Daniels, Steve and Louise Campbell Tolber, Donna and Hal Hankinson, Robin and John Rubel, Jane and John Bagwell, Sarah and

Doug Brown, Ashley and Paul Margetson, Mary and Alex Ross, Natalie Fitz-Gerald, Cherie and Michael Gamble, Sandy and Russ Osterman, Jeri and Philip Hertzman, Mara and Chuck Robinson, Susan and Karl Horn, Kathy and Bob Reidy, Helene Pfeffer, Donna and Jack Rust, Jane Ann and Jasper Welch, Gina Browning, Joe Illick, and of course Dianne and Don Chalmers. There are so many more good friends, but I would need to add another ten pages to this book. A note to tell all of you whom I did not name, I am most grateful for your friendship and companionship.

We have been members of Beit Tikva temple for many years and our small temple has been a source of joy and solace. We are very pleased with the new rabbi, Martin Levy, and have enjoyed our Friday night Sabbath services. Through Beit Tikva, we have funded the Richard and Eleanor Brenner Educational Series in 2010, which features simulcast lectures from the 92nd Street Y in New York. It has been very well received in the community.

People come here to live and not to enter a retirement community waiting to die. The people who come here are doers and very involved and continue their involvement here or even expand their activities. The people who come have been very successful in their fields of endeavor but do not wear their success on their sleeve. They rarely talk about their successes but are more concerned with maintaining the beauty of New Mexico and with what is going on in our community, state, country, and world. As I mentioned earlier, they are very charitable of their time, thoughts, and money, and constantly give to the many non-profits that exist in Santa Fe.

Above all, people reach out to make friends. They are not cloistered in a small intimate group. Rather, you have good friends from all over the city, and in fact the state, with varying interests and political positions. It is the easiest place for a single person to live because they are included and treated just the same as couples. We have made great close friends who would extend themselves for us as we would extend ourselves for them. Everyone knows about the Opera, the galleries and southwestern art, chamber music and the Concert Association, lectures and live performances and all the cultural and artistic things that are part of Santa Fe. The area is very sports-driven, from fishing to hiking to golf to tennis. It is common to see people smile at each other as you pass and people respond by saying to each other how lucky they are to live in such a place or that they live in paradise. All this I throw into the hopper and something additional, that I call the "Mystique of Santa Fe"—the intangible that makes this such a great place to live with great friends. I hope that GOD grants me sufficient time to continue to enjoy this wonderful Santa Fe and our many dear friends.

My thanks and appreciation for the outstanding assistance and editing performed by Maddie Schryer, Anthony Brenner, and John Rubel.

And, of course, my wife Eleanor P. Brenner edited and wrote several sections such as descriptions of the India and Africa parties as well as the Executive Woman. Her prodigious memory was a great asset in remembering the past.

Thank you all for helping me to achieve my vision of *My Life Seen Through Our Eyes*.

www.ingramcontent.com/pod-product-compliance
Lightning Source LLC
Chambersburg PA
CBHW020454100426
42813CB00031B/3364/J